Model Railroad

MODEL RAILROAD HANDBOOK NO. 37

Electronics

Basic Concepts to Advanced Projects

by Peter J. Thorne

KALMBACH BOOKS

Project Editor: George Drury
Copy Editor: Mary Algozin
Art and Layout: Sabine Beaupré, Chris Farris
Cover Photo: Jim Forbes

Publisher's Cataloging in Publication
(Prepared by Quality Books Inc.)

Thorne, Peter J.
    Model railroad electronics : basic concepts to advanced
projects
    / Peter J. Thorne.
        p. cm. — (Model railroad handbook ; 37)
        Includes index.
        ISBN 0-89024-146-5

    1. Railroads--Models--Electronic equipment. I. Title. II.
Series

    TF197.T536 1994   625.1'9
                                              QBI94-1320

Contents

1 Basic electronic answers

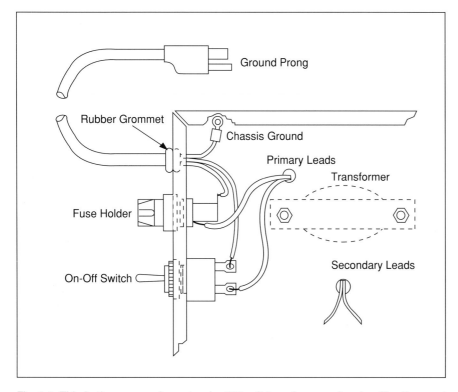

Fig. 1-1. This is the approved way to wire 110-volt transformer primaries. The line cord must be securely attached to the case to eliminate any chance of pulling wires out.

Ground Prong

Rubber Grommet

Chassis Ground

Primary Leads

Transformer

Fuse Holder

On-Off Switch

Secondary Leads

THREE ITEMS are of concern to the model railroader working with electronics: safety, sources of components, and special techniques. Safety is important. Electricity is unforgiving of mistakes, particularly when you are working with 110-volt household electricity down in the basement surrounded by water pipes, exposed electrical conduits, and masonry walls and floor, all at ground potential.

Some components are hard to find. Electronics is a rapidly evolving science. Some parts that were readily available five years ago have disappeared. Even large corporations such as Radio Shack change their mix of components annually. This chapter should reduce the pain and surprise.

Special techniques are necessary

to install and use electronics on model railroads. Printed circuits are a necessity when using integrated circuits and small-size transistors. This chapter contains instructions for making your own printed circuit boards (PC boards). Some components are tiny and fragile; they require special handling and soldering techniques.

What is necessary for safety?

A model railroad must be isolated from the 110-volt AC power in the wall socket. Commercial electrical devices must conform to safety standards. Injury or death can result from touching a live wire and having another part of your body grounded at the same time. The maximum safe voltage for use on a model railroad is about 30

volts. Be aware that a fuse in the power line in no way guarantees human (or pet) safety. The typical 15-ampere fuse or circuit breaker limit is to prevent fire, not personal electric shock. To look at it another way, the amount of current sufficient to kill you isn't nearly enough to trip the breaker or blow the fuse.

A ground fault interrupter (GFI) is a replacement for the standard duplex wall plug. It contains sensitive electronics and a fast relay that disconnects the power if there is as little as 0.0002 ampere of leakage. Since 1986 electrical codes have required that kitchen, bathroom, basement, and outdoor power outlets be protected with GFIs. GFIs are a wise idea in your hobby room too. They are a standard hardware-store item costing about $10, and they are not difficult to install. Follow the instructions packaged with them—starting by turning off the power to the circuit at the breaker or fuse box. The type that is connected by pushing in the leads may be too deep for outlet boxes in older houses; use the kind with screw terminals.

Another area where safety is a concern is the wiring of transformers. Fig. 1-1 shows exactly how a power transformer must be wired to comply with safety codes. You should note also that the transformer itself should be marked as approved by Underwriters Laboratories (UL) in the United States and Canadian Standards Association (CSA) in Canada. The transformer isolates the potentially dangerous line voltage from your low-voltage motors, lights, and switch machines.

Another way to be safe is to use a wall-socket-mounted transformer, as shown in fig. 1-2. These transformers are intended for continuous operation to power such items as telephone answering machines, but I suggest you use them only in wall sockets controlled by an on-off switch. If you leave your layout for a time, they and whatever they power can then be turned off before you close the door.

Another route to safety is to use a spare or retired train power pack as your low-voltage source. Two throttle circuits in Chapter 4 illustrate this. Power packs that have no on-off switch should be plugged into sockets that can be switched off.

What is the easiest way to purchase components?

In previous books I have suggested Radio Shack as the preferred source of components, but their range of components has shrunk considerably in recent years. If a part is likely to be available from Radio Shack, that is noted in the parts lists in this book.

The best source is mail-order retailers such as Mouser Electronics, Digi-Key Corporation, and Jameco Electronics. Their addresses and phone numbers appear in the list of suppliers at the back of this book. The monthly magazine *Electronics Now* can be found on newsstands. It contains numerous advertisements for components. Some electronics suppliers advertise in *Model Railroader*.

The third (and least accessible) source is the industrial electronic component distributors. They are listed in the Yellow Pages. Three of the largest are Hamilton Hallmark, Aimac Arrow Electronics, and Future Electronics. Future has a division called Active Components, which caters to the smaller-volume user and also offers a catalog. All of these mentioned also operate in Canada. Others with nationwide outlets include Bell Industries, Marshall Industries, Newark Electronics, and Time Electronics. Some branches of these nationwide distributors offer walk-in counter sales. In Canada, Electrosonic has a walk-in counter, at least at their head location in Toronto. Active Components has several counter locations across Canada and the U.S. In a few cases the parts lists in this book give phone or fax numbers for specific component manufacturers. All will supply you with the name of a distributor but will not supply you directly.

How do I solder small items?

You need a pencil-type iron with a fine tip and a 25- to 45-watt element. The Weller 35-watt pencil iron with a

Fig. 1-2. A safe way to connect to AC power. These units plug into a wall socket. A variety of voltages is available. Choose 12 to 16 volts AC for most model railroad applications.

Fig. 1-3. A ground fault interrupter (GFI) ensures that the layout is safe electrically.

Fig. 1-4. A good solder joint is a glossy bead, not a crystalline lump. Surviving a good tug is also a measure of soldering quality.

⅛" screwdriver tip is particularly good (Mouser catalog 561, part number 576-WP35). Radio Shack 64-8071 (1993 catalog) is a 45-watt unit that is also suitable. This type of iron is also ideal for soldering feeder wires to rails. See fig. 1-4. You also need a holder and wettable hot-tip wiper (Radio Shack 64-2078; Mouser 578-PH60). Radio Shack No. 64-2801 is a complete electronics kit with a 30-watt iron, interchangeable tips, solder, stand, wire cutters, pliers, and screwdrivers.

Never use a soldering gun for small parts, though a gun is useful for soldering heavy-gauge copper wire for block or turnout wires. Underneath the layout is a good place for screw terminals instead of solder connections—if for no other reason than to avoid the hazards of soldering overhead. Who needs a drop of hot solder on the nose?

Parts being soldered must be clean. Don't rely on the resin flux in the solder wire to clean up dust, dirt, or grease. The key to successful small-part soldering is to heat the work, not just the solder. Don't carry the solder to the job on the tip of the iron. Heat the joint and apply the 60/40 solder. (It's in the form of a thin wire.) Heat it fast until the molten solder forms a shiny puddle, then remove the iron.

The term 60/40 for electronic solder means 60 percent tin and 40 percent lead. Solder for plumbing contains no lead because of the hazard of lead in contact with drinking water, but this is not a hazard for our application. The lead content results in a low-melting-point solder that solidifies rapidly. This solder contains non-corrosive resin flux instead of acid flux.

Remember that transistors and diodes can be damaged by too much heat for too long. Cooling clips can keep the wire cool but get in the way.

Among the more difficult items to solder are power transformer leads (which are thick copper) and integrated-circuit sockets (leads are small and very close together). With the latter it's likely that solder bridges will form between adjacent copper pads. You can usually clear the bridges by briskly shaking the board (away from you) while the solder is still molten—you have only a couple of seconds to do it. If that doesn't do the job, pick it away with a knife.

What is a printed circuit board?

Why is it required?

A printed circuit board (PC board) consists of a sheet of hard plastic with a thin layer of copper on one side. Most of the copper is removed, leaving circuit paths that substitute for flexible wire. Circuit components are mounted on the board, usually with their leads pushed through holes drilled in the board and soldered to copper areas. PC boards are necessary for circuits consisting of many small components with short leads, particularly integrated circuits with short pins close together.

That's not to say that the devices using PC boards in this book can't be made by other methods, such as wire-wrap, but they require more skill and are more mistake-prone than using a PC board. In Chapter 2 is a circuit that uses a generic PC board.

How is a PC board made?

After paths that will serve as the wires of the circuit are masked, the rest of the copper is removed chemically. Holes are drilled for the component leads to go through the panel and into the copper paths, where they are soldered.

It follows that the layout is fixed, and there is no later flexibility of positioning the components. On the other hand, it's easier to avoid mistakes in placement and wiring of components.

Where can I get PC board material?

Your first choice most likely will be Radio Shack part No. 276-170, a 5⁷⁄₁₆" × 2⁷⁄₁₆" board. Otherwise get FR-1 or FR-4 PC board material, ¹⁄₁₆" thick, plated with copper on one side only, such as Mouser 501-PC12×12, which is a 12" square sheet. This is a general-purpose grade, used everywhere in electronics. Most distributors carry it.

Is there an easy way to make printed circuit boards?

No. The setup time necessary for automated manufacture of PC boards makes small quantities prohibitively expensive. If you need two or three you will have to make them by hand. Fortunately, only complex circuits need PC boards, and often an existing product already on a PC board can be modified. There are some examples in later chapters.

How do I make a PC board?

Figs. 1-5 through 1-9 illustrate one

technique. Using the foil-side diagrams in this book, first cut a piece of board to the required dimensions. Cut through the copper with a sharp knife, scribe the blank side on the same line, then snap the piece off—the same technique as cutting sheet styrene.

Place the foil-side diagram on the copper side of the board. Prick through all the hole centers with a sharp scriber or compass point, then remove the diagram and center-punch the hole centers. Drill the holes with a No. 60 to No. 65 bit in a motor tool or the equivalent. Some holes may need to be enlarged for the components, but wait until the board has been etched.

Clean the copper side of the board thoroughly with detergent, wetted household scouring powder, or 600-grit emery paper. Using the foil-side diagram in the book, draw the paths that connect the holes. You will need a special pen with solvent-resistant black ink, such as Mouser 524-22-220. Special care is needed for closely spaced connections, like those for integrated circuits, because the hole centers are just 0.1" apart.

You may be able to obtain sets of dry transfer patterns for integrated circuits and straight and curved lines. Radio Shack 276-1577 was discontinued for a couple of years but was once again available in 1993. Radio Shack 276-1576 is a complete PC board kit including rub-on transfers, etchant, tank, and pen with resistant ink. Datak Products offers a full range of dry transfer items, plus transfers for panels and meters. You can get them through Jameco Electronics.

I've found it possible to hand-copy a simple board (it's impractical for boards with closely spaced traces) using marking pens. Sanford Sharpie Permanent Markers resist ferric chloride; other brands may work too. I apply two layers, baking the coated PC board in the oven at 200 degrees for two minutes between layers. After etching you can scrub off the ink readily with either acetone (nail polish remover—buy your own instead of borrowing it) or scouring powder and hot water.

A third short cut may still be available. Copy the circuit pattern in the book onto a sheet of TEC-200 film, using a plain photocopier. Next iron the film onto the copper side of the PC board. Then peel off the film and etch. At the time of writing the film was available from DC Electronics and Ocean State Electronics.

After applying the resist ink, the next step is to etch away the unwanted copper in the area not covered by the resist ink. Two etchants work well, ferric chloride and ammonium persulfate. Ferric chloride is a dark green liquid. Part numbers are Radio Shack 276-1535 (16 ounces, enough for most projects) and Mouser 503-FECL-B (1 gallon). Ammonium persulfate (Mouser 503-APS-B) consists of white crystals to be dissolved in hot water before use. One pound makes a gallon of etchant.

Pour about half an inch into a shallow glass or plastic shallow dish, and immerse the board in the etchant. If the copper side is up, you can keep an eye on the process, but be sure that the board remains completely immersed.

Agitate the container gently from time to time. Etching will take 5 to 15 minutes, depending on the temperature and concentration. The ammonium persulfate turns blue as it removes copper; ferric chloride remains the same color.

Heating the ammonium persulfate in a glass or plastic container in a microwave oven—no more than 60 seconds at heat level 4 or "defrost"—makes it work faster. Do not heat ferric chloride. It gives off chlorine. Whichever etchant you use, your work area must be well ventilated.

When the board is fully etched, take it out of the etchant and rinse it thoroughly. Remove all ink and dry transfer material with lacquer thinner or acetone. Clean and dry thoroughly before inserting components and soldering.

Deburr the holes with emery cloth. Don't use a countersink drill for this, because it will remove some of the soldering surface. You can reuse the etchant if you have etched only a small board.

What safety precautions are necessary?

Handle the etchants, lacquer thinner, and acetone with rubber gloves. Do not flush any of the chemicals into the sewers. Don't put them into metal

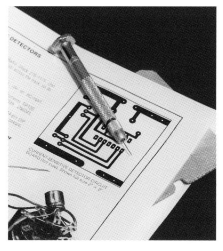

Fig. 1-5. Mark the component location holes. The point goes through the paper to the copper-foil side of the PC board

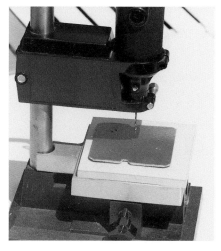

Fig. 1-6. Drill the holes for the components. The PC board has not been etched.

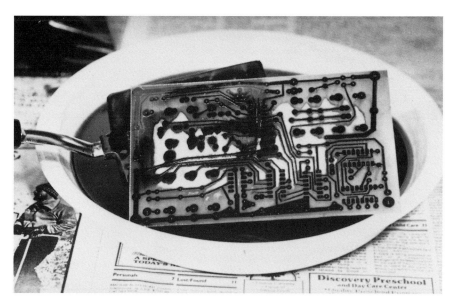

Fig. 1-7. Etch away the copper not required for conduction paths. Datak Corp photo.

Fig. 1-8. After etching, remove the dry transfer etch resist with mineral spirits or acetone. Datak Corp. photo.

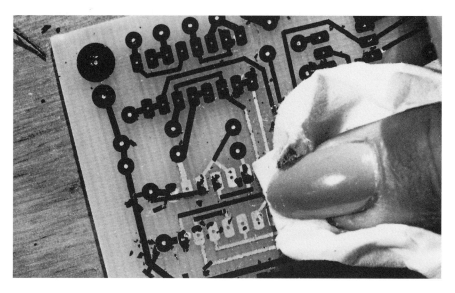

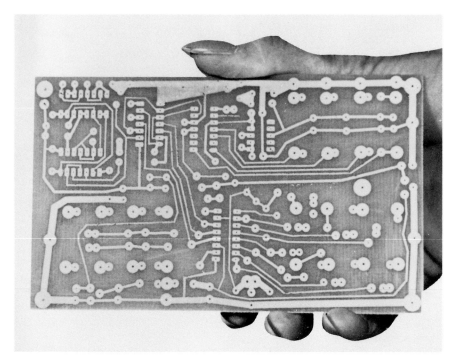

Fig. 1-9. A finished board. Datak Corp. photo.

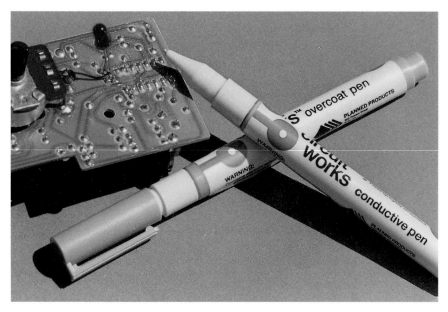

Fig. 1-10. Board repair using silver conductive ink. This is useful if excess etching time has eroded the copper areas.

containers. Ventilate your work area well during the etching and cleaning processes.

If I make a mistake in drawing or etch too long, can I repair the board?

Mouser part 527-2200 is a pen that makes a conductive repair path, and Mouser 527-3300G is a similar pen that lays down a protective coating to keep the conductive path from corroding. See fig. 1-10. You could make a simple PC board using just these pens, without the need for etchant.

I need several identical boards. How can I mass-produce them?

Kits are available from Mouser (No. 524-22-312) and Newark (Kepro Circuit Systems No. FK-701). The latter enables you to make PC boards in quantity by using a photosensitized film that needs no darkroom or special developing lights. Most distributors carry similar complete kits; all have full instructions. The Kepro is probably the easiest to use.

I'd like to make just one board as a minimum-cost experiment. What do you suggest?

It is possible to grind away copper areas using a fine grinding wheel in a motor tool. It requires skill and is impossible when integrated circuit pads are involved. Try the flasher circuit board in Chapter 2 as a starter. Wear eye protection when grinding.

Component symbols

The next page shows the standard symbols for electronic components that are used in this book. Most of these symbols are really illustrative: two-wire components show two leads; a transistor has three; the symbols for switches and pushbuttons resemble what they do.

ABBREVIATIONS

A	Amp, ampere	E	Emitter (of transistor)	mW	Milliwatt = 0.001 watt
AC	Alternating current	Hz	Hertz (cycles per second)	SCR	Silicon controlled rectifier, thyristor
B	Base (of transistor)	K	Kilohm = 1000 ohms	SPST	Single-pole, single-throw (switch)
C	Collector (of transistor)	KHz	Kilohertz = 1000 hertz	W	Watts
DC	Direct current	LED	Light-emitting diode	μF	Microfarad
DPDT	Double-pole, double-throw (switch)	M	Megohm = 1,000,000 ohms	Ω	Ohm

SYMBOLS

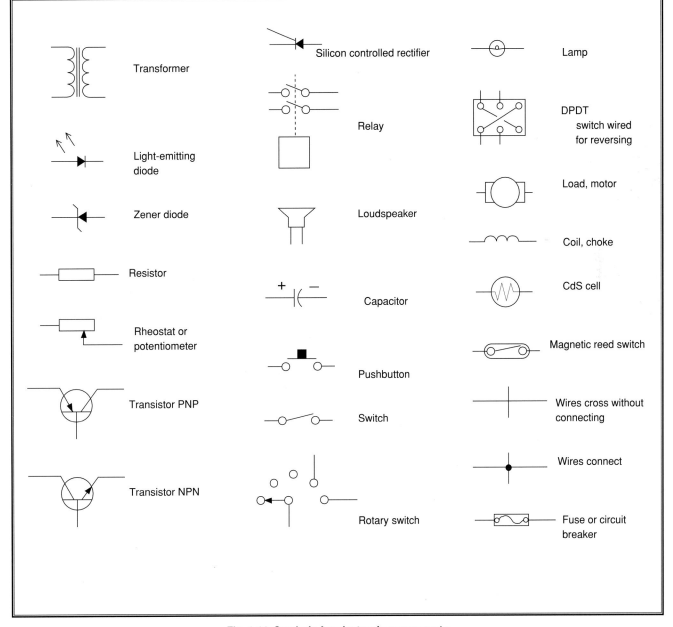

Fig. 1-11. Symbols for electronic components.

2 Lamps, lights, and illumination

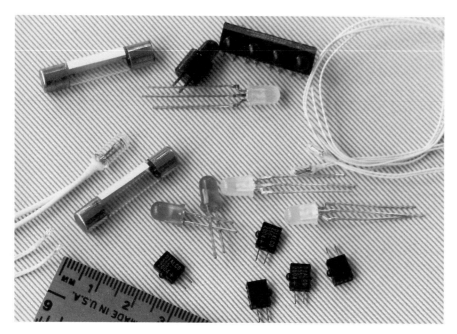

Fig. 2-1. Incandescent lamp and LED packages run from 2 mm to 7 mm in diameter.

WHILE SCENERY and accuracy of scale are the principal components of realism in a model railroad, lighting of models and details often gives a boost to realism. Lights are easy to install and understand. One circuit in this chapter is a simple dimmer for small grain-of-wheat bulbs; another can perform several "moving light" functions. You'll find a straightforward flasher circuit that can operate any number or types of lamps, as well as a solution to problems that can occur with some locomotive lighting circuits. In addition, there are several circuits for room lighting and special effects, so you can simulate dusk, dawn, and noon, adding to the satisfaction of train, building, and signal illumination.

What's the difference between an ordinary small light bulb and a light-emitting diode (LED)?

The small light bulb used as head-lamp in most model locomotives and cars is made the same way as a household incandescent light. Sealed in a glass bulb is a tungsten filament, which becomes white-hot when electricity passes through it. The household lamp is powered from 110-volt alternating current and consumes from 15 to 250 watts of power; model lamps are rated for 1.5 to 16 volts alternating or direct current (AC or DC), and consume less than 1 watt.

Incandescent lamps are inefficient, releasing most of their power as heat. Have you ever tried to change a 100-watt lamp without gloves just after switching it off?

Light-emitting diodes are more efficient. They operate on 1.5- to 5-volt DC at around 0.3 watt (300 milliwatts). They do not work on AC, except for one special type described below. They are available in red, yellow, green, and (more expensive) blue. They must be connected in the correct polarity (anode to +; cathode to -). Incandescents can be connected either way and give a yellow to white light. LEDs have no fragile filament and are thus more rugged; they last at least ten times longer than incandescent bulbs.

Where are the best places to use LEDs?

Consider color. Red, yellow, and green LEDs are naturals for signals. They cannot reproduce either the white light of fluorescent lighting or the yellow-white of incandescents, but yellow LEDs can simulate floor and table lamps in buildings.

Among the special LEDs are a self-flashing red and, useful for a signal lamp, a two-color unit that is red with one polarity and green with the other. If you apply AC, the red and green alternate to make yellow. LEDs can be destroyed by voltage over the maximum permitted (usually 2 to 3 volts), though flashers take 5 to 9 volts, and blue LEDs are rated as high as 9 volts or so.

Where are the best places for incandescents?

Model incandescent lamps are at their best when they simulate prototype incandescents in buildings, houses, passenger cars, and locomotive headlights.

Consider also brightness and angle of view. LEDs are not normally as bright as incandescents, and many give little light to the side. If you view signals from oblique angles when running your railroad, LED signals may not be visible except from close to head-on.

Commercial signals nearly always use tinted 16-volt incandescents, for one good reason: LEDs need a series resistor to operate safely from the DC power pack output, while incandescents need no voltage-limiting resistor

Fig. 2-2. Incandescent lamps in series (above) and in parallel (below).

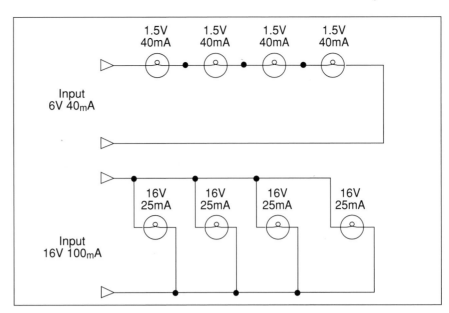

and can operate from the 16-volt AC terminals of a power pack.

What is series wiring?

Fig. 2-2 shows lamps connected in series. Series connection reduces the wiring needed in model buildings, but the drawback is that when one lamp in the string burns out the circuit is broken and none of the lamps will light. (Many Christmas tree lights are wired in series.)

The rule for series connection is that the voltage is divided among the lamps and all draw the same current (amps). It's best if all lamps also have the same voltage and current ratings, though you can break this rule if you want one lamp in the chain to be brighter than the others.

Series connection is useful if your available lamps are of lower voltage than your power supply voltage. Thus you can connect three 6-volt lamps in series (they total 18 volts) to a 16-volt AC power pack. A side benefit is that the lamps will last longer because they are getting slightly less than their rated voltage. If you want to add more lamps, connect another set of three series-connected lamps in parallel with the first set—but first read the next question and answer!

How does parallel connection differ from series?

In fig. 2-2 you can also see that in parallel connection the two leads of each lamp are connected directly to the power supply. Each lamp therefore must be rated at the power supply voltage. All the lamps must be the same voltage, but they may have different current ratings. The total power supply load will be the sum of all the lamp currents.

Can I use 12-volt lamps on a 16-volt supply without blowing them?

You could use pairs of them in series. Each get 8 volts. They would be dim but possibly satisfactory, and their life would be doubled.

The alternative, often used with LEDs, is to wire a resistor in series with each lamp—see fig. 2-3. Now we have to become technicians and refer to Ohm's Law: Voltage equals current multiplied by resistance (volts equals amps times ohms) or resistance equals

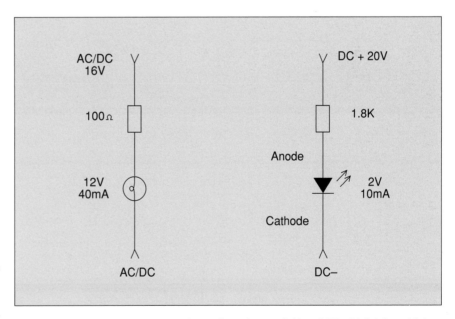

Fig. 2-3. Resistors are used to run low-voltage lamps (left) or LEDs (right) from higher-voltage supplies.

voltage divided by current (ohms equals volts divided by amps).

You need to drop 4 volts from the 16-volt supply before it hits the 12-volt lamp. Let's say the lamp current is 40 milliamps, which is typical. That's 0.04 amperes (we'll call them amps from now on). The resistance for 4 volts at 0.04 amps is 4 divided by 0.04. That's 100 ohms. Wiring a 100-ohm resistor in series with a 12-volt lamp enables it to burn at full brightness from a 16-volt supply without popping.

The resistor wastes the excess voltage as heat, and the capacity of the

resistor is measured in watts—volts times amps. In this case it's 4 × 0.04 = 0.16 watt. A 0.25-watt resistor is sufficient. There's no harm in using a 0.5-watt resistor (the excess capacity costs money, of course), but a 0.125-watt resistor (usually called one-eighth-watt) would overheat.

What about LEDs in series and parallel?

LEDs are almost always wired in parallel with each other, but since they are mostly 2-volt devices, you almost always need a resistor in series

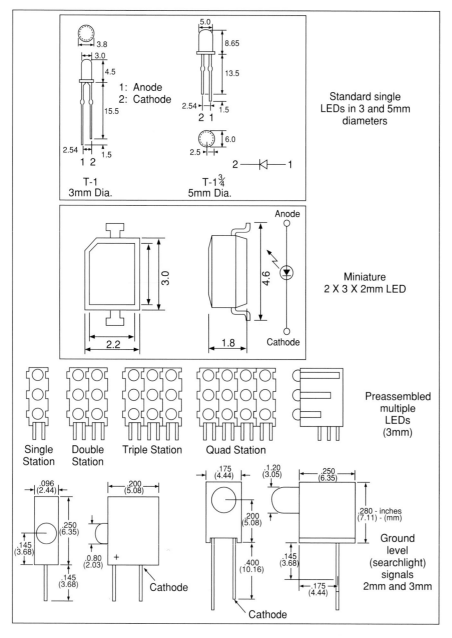

Fig. 2-4. Standard, miniature, and signal packages for LEDs. Some are available with built-in resistors for 5-or 12-volt power.

with the LED. Most LEDs run at 10 milliamps, some at 20 milliamps, and some efficient, high-brightness types at 2 milliamps. As a rule of thumb assume 10 milliamps, but if you need a brighter light, figure on 18 milliamps. A quick calculation at 10 milliamps gives a series resistor of 300 ohms for a 5-volt supply, 1,000 ohms for a 12-volt supply, and 2,000 ohms (2K) for a 22-volt supply. A 0.25 watt resistor does for all.

The reason for mentioning 22 volts instead of 16 is that LEDs require DC, not AC. If you use a 16-volt AC power supply for LEDs, its output must be rectified and filtered, and the resulting DC voltage is between 22 and 25 (for an explanation of how 16 volts turns into 22 to 25 volts, see the section on transformers in Chapter 3.

How can I dim building lamps?

If you're using AC, placing a diode in series with each lamp or group of lamps will halve the brightness. Fig. 2-6 shows the wiring. The diode blocks the current in one direction, so the lamps receive current only half the time. There is no heat to dissipate, as there would be with a resistor, so the diode is in effect a "wattless resistor." The switch bypasses the diode for full brightness.

Can the wattless dropper be used with lamps in command control systems?

It will work with command control systems that have AC in the rails. The Zero-1 and the Kato Digital systems each use a form of AC across the rails, far too much for the lamps in engines and cars. Adding the diode in series with the lamp cuts the effective voltage to the lamp to 9 volts while maintaining constant brightness. See fig. 2-7. Unlike a resistor, the diode drops voltage without creating heat, so it won't endanger plastic parts.

This doesn't apply to command control systems with DC on the rails.

Fig. 2-5. Bicolor (red and green) LED can be used for signals by reversing the DC polarity (left) or by a switch with the 3-lead device (right).

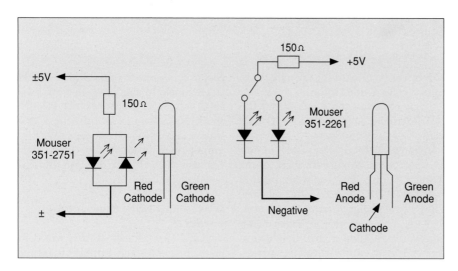

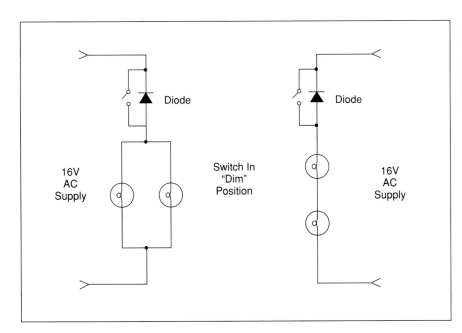

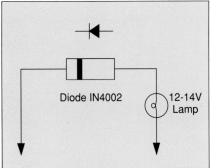

Fig. 2-6. Using a switch and a diode to reduce the brightness of incandescent lamps for buildings or yards. Diode polarity does not matter here.

Fig. 2-7. The diode dimmer is also used to prevent burnout of locomotive lights for AC-track-powered command control systems such as the Zero-1 or Kato Digital.

How can LEDs be used for signals?

Commercially available signals for the most part use colored 16-volt incandescent lamps, which are somewhat large for N scale. LED assemblies are available in both 2 mm and 3 mm sizes. The smaller size equals 12 inches in N; the larger, about 10 inches in HO. They're designed to be used as indicators on printed circuit assemblies and are called circuit board indicators, but they're ideal for use as signals. For dwarf signals they can be used unadorned; for high signals [note to me: check term in Cyc] they will need a mast and a target, which can be made easily.

Dialight offers a 2 mm right-angle single lamp: no. 555-2001 in red, 555-2401 in yellow, and 555-2301 in green. Current is 20 milliamps at 1.6 to 2.2 volts. The 3 mm right-angle singles are 551-0407 in red, -0307 in yellow, and -0207 in green. Current is 10 milliamps at 2.0 to 2.1 volts.

Dialight offers a 3 mm triple vertical stack unit with red, yellow, and green lights suitable for railroad or highway traffic signals, no. 564-0100-132. Current is 10 milliamps at 2.2 volts; it is a very bright unit. Triple stacks are also available in all-red and all-green.

Most major distributors such as Mouser Electronics can supply similar units.

What is the single-unit red-green LED mentioned earlier?

Dialight no. 550-3008 is a 5 mm single unit that is bright red with DC in one direction and bright green in the other. AC produces yellow (AC is permissible because the unit actually contains two LEDs, one connected in each direction). Current is 10 milliamps at 1.75–2.0 volts.

Marktech offers unmounted LEDs of this type. The 5 mm version is no. MT5491-HRG; 3 mm, MT2030-HRG. Some red-green LEDs have three leads (a common cathode and anodes for red and green). Examples are Marktech MT6203-HRG (3 mm) and MT6226-HRG (5 mm).

The signal circuit using these dual-color LEDs is on page 58 of *34 New Electronic Projects for Model Railroaders.*

What about self-flashing LEDs?

These are available in red, green, and yellow. Radio Shack's 276-016 is a red 5-volt unit in a 5 mm package with two wires. Marktech's 9-volt MT-605 series is available in three colors. Mouser offers Lytron Devices 5-volt flashers (451-50001, -50020, and -50031 in red, green, and yellow respectively). All three brands are 5 mm. They are too large for use as roof flashers in N scale; even in HO they are 17 scale inches. It may be possible

Fig. 2-8. The flasher circuit board.

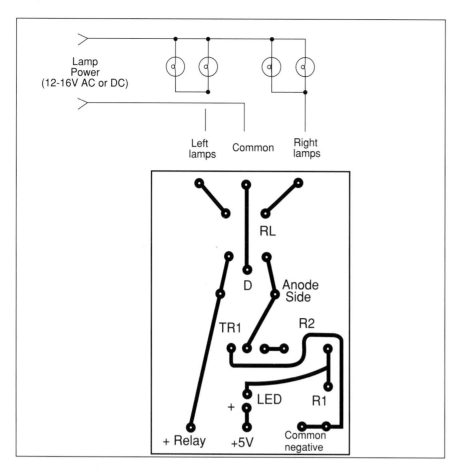

to mount the entire flasher inside the hood and conduct the light through a smaller diameter rod of transparent plastic. A stable filtered DC power source of 5 volts for the flasher LED is still needed. You'll find such a circuit in 34 New Electronic Projects for Model Railroaders. Elsewhere in this book is a circuit that flashes an ordinary LED of any diameter and operates on 1.5 volts.

Using a self-flashing LED to drive a highway crossing flasher

A flashing LED can be used to switch a transistor on and off. In the circuit of fig. 2-10, the transistor in turn operates a relay. Although the flashing LED only goes on and off, the relay can switch one set of lights on when the LED is off, and the other set on when the LED is on. Most LED flashers operate at 1.5 to 2.5 times a second.

The circuit shows separate power supplies for flasher and the relay, but if you use a 5-volt relay, they can use the same 5-volt supply. The crossing lights are completely separate and can be powered from the appropriate source. If you use LEDs for crossing lights, you can use the same 5-volt power source as the relay and the flasher, but you will need to connect a 220-ohm, 0.25-watt resistor in series with each LED.

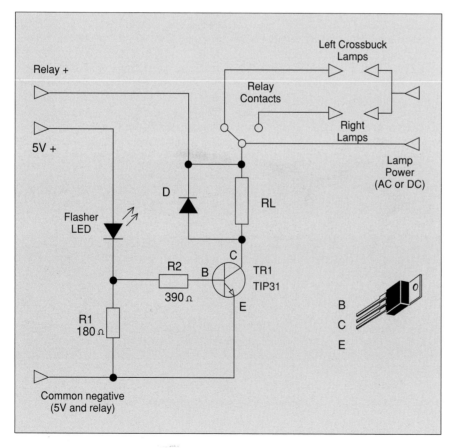

Fig. 2-10. Circuit of the flasher unit.

PARTS LIST FOR FLASHER (FIG. 2-10)	
LED flasher	5-volt type: Radio Shack 276-016; Mouser 351-50001
R1	180-ohm, 0.25-watt resistor
R2	390-ohm, 0.25-watt resistor
D	1N4004 diode
TR1	NPN Transistor, TIP29 or TIP31
RL	Relay with 5-, 9-, or 12-volt coil and SPDT contacts (1 Form C). Radio Shack 275-241 is 12 volt. Mouser 431-1305 is 5 volt. Digi-Key Z100-ND is 5 volt.
Miscellaneous	
	Terminal stakes or wire for connections Copper-clad PCB material. The circuit board will need to be revised to fit the relay you select. Alternately, short wires can be soldered from the original circuit board connections to the new relay.

Fig. 2-11. Constant locomotive lighting. Diodes must be rated at motor current—for example, 1N4002 for HO or N; 1N5402 for O or G scales.

If the flasher LED is on your control panel, it can give a visual indication of when the circuit is operating, or you can let it flash unseen beneath the layout. Choose a small relay, as specified in the parts list, to minimize clicking noise while it is operating. Take care to connect the transistor and the diode correctly. If either is reversed the circuit will not operate.

Are LEDs bright enough to use for locomotive headlights?

In general, no, at least until recently. But LEDs are top technology, and research is under way to increase the light output. Hewlett-Packard Components' HLMA-DL00 is a 2-volt, 20-milliamp yellow LED that can throw a beam in daylight. It's ideal for a headlight. The light output is some 100 times greater than the typical general-purpose LED. Fig. 2-11 gives a circuit using the HLMA-DL00 as an automatic headlight that is on when the engine is running forward.

I installed a commercial constant-lighting kit in a locomotive with a can motor, and the headlight glows only dimly. What's wrong?

Constant lighting circuits rely on a constant 0.7-volt drop across diodes connected in series with the motor (fig. 2-11). Two diodes in series make 1.4 volts available for a lamp; three, 2.1 volts. This voltage is subtracted from the voltage the motor gets. If the power pack supplies 8 volts and there are two diodes in series with the motor, the motor gets 8 minus 2.1 volts.

The catch with an efficient motor is that the lamp current must be less than the motor current. It isn't scientifically possible for a lamp in series with a motor (regardless of diodes) to draw more current than the motor. If you try to use a 1.5-volt, 90-milliamp lamp in a constant lighting circuit when the motor draws only 50 milliamps, the lamp is dim. If the motor draws 300 milliamps—more typical—there is no problem. Most of the current goes through the diodes, leaving plenty for the lamp. The high-brightness LED will work with all motors because it needs but 10 to 20 milliamps to light.

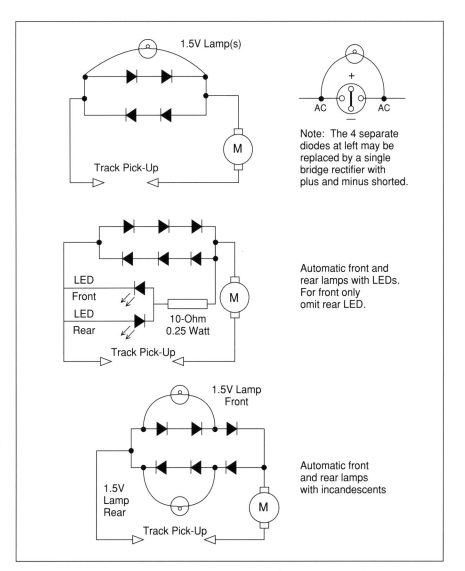

Note: The 4 separate diodes at left may be replaced by a single bridge rectifier with plus and minus shorted.

Automatic front and rear lamps with LEDs. For front only omit rear LED.

Automatic front and rear lamps with incandescents

Fig. 2-12. The high light output Hewlett-Packard LED is an effective headlamp for HO (right). The locomotive on the left uses four 1.5-volt, 15-milliamp incandescent lamps to light its way.

15

Then it's not possible to have multiple constant headlights on one locomotive?

You can have as many lamps as add up to the slow-running motor current. Incandescent lamps are available with currents as low as 15 milliamps at 1.5 volts. Four to six of these lamps can be used off one set of constant-lighting diodes with most motors. Two high-brightness LEDs can be used with automatic front-rear switching.

In the circuit shown in fig. 2-11, only one of the lamps is on at a time (forward or reverse), so not more than 30 milliamps is needed. Note that some current must go through the diodes, so add 20 milliamps to the total of all lamp currents when checking whether the grand total is less than the slow-running motor current.

Making electronic chase lights

Chase lights are an elegant addition to the marquee of a theater on the layout. This circuit will light ten LEDs one after the other. The speed can be fast, or as slow as one per second. Although the integrated circuits will deliver only enough current (10 milliamps) to light LEDs, I've included an interface circuit for incandescent lamps (from 40 to 300 milliamps) in case you prefer to use these in place of LEDs. You need one transistor and one resistor per lamp. No heat sink is required for the transistor that accommodates the cold surge current of the lamp filament.

Fig. 2-13 gives details of the circuit, which is constructed on a PC board that you don't have to make—it's prefabricated by Radio Shack.

The assembly steps are as follows. I used several colors of wire to help me check the wiring after completion.

❏ Insert the two IC sockets (install the ICs last).

❏ With black wire connect pin 1 of U1, pin 8 of U2, pin 13, and pin 15 to the negative power source lead.

❏ With blue wire join pin 2 to pin 6 of U1.

❏ With yellow wire join pin 3 of U1 to pin 14 of U2.

❏ With green wire join pin 4 to pin 8 of U1.

❏ With purple wire join pin 8 of U1 and pin 16 of U2 to the on-off switch.

❏ Connect the other side of the on-off switch to the positive power source.

(Note there are no connections to pin 5 of U1 or to pin 12 of U2.)

❏ Connect R1 (1K; brown-black-red) from pin 8 of U2 to a brown flexible lead that goes to the cathodes of all ten LEDs.

❏ Connect R2 (10K; brown-black-orange) between pins 7 and 8 of U1.

❏ Connect R3 (1M; brown-black-green) between pins 2 and 7 of U1.

(The three resistors, like the wires, are inserted from the top of the PC board. The two capacitors are connected at the bottom of the PC board.)

❏ Connect C1 (0.22µF) between pins 15 and 16 of U2.

❏ Connect C2 (see parts list) between pins 1 and 2 of U1.

❏ Using a convenient length of 10-conductor ribbon cable, connect the anodes (positive leads) of the ten LEDs to the indicated pin numbers of U2. Note the pin numbers carefully if you want the LEDs to light in sequence. (Ribbon cable often comes in 14-leads,

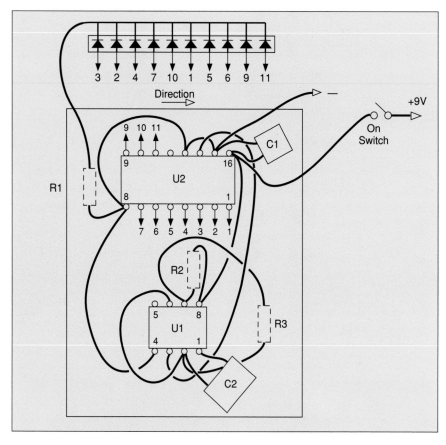

Fig. 2-13. Wiring of chase light from copper side. Note all wires and resistors are on the top side together with the ICs. Pin numbering above is as seen on the bottom of the ICs. Refer to photos when wiring.

PARTS LIST FOR CHASE LIGHTS (FIG. 2-13)

U1	NE555N analog timer integrated circuit
U2	CD4017BE or MC14017BCP digital decade counter IC
R1	1K, 0.25-watt resistor
R2	10K, 0.25-watt resistor
R3	1-megohm, 0.25-watt resistor
C1	0.22µF, 50-volt (or higher) film or ceramic capacitor (no special tolerance requirement)
C2	0.1µF gives complete chase time of 1 second for the ten LEDs; 1µF gives 1 second per lamp. 0.22µF is a happy medium. Film or ceramic 10% tolerance capacitor, 50-volt or higher
Miscellaneous	Circuit board: Radio Shack 276-158
	8-pin and 16-pin IC sockets
	10 LEDs
	Single pole on-off switch
	Length of ribbon cable to connect the LEDs

Fig. 2-14. (Right) Top of the chase light circuit board.

Fig. 2-15. (Far right) View of bottom of chase light board.

but it is easy to knife off the extras. There's no reason not to use separate wires, apart from convenience and appearance). I inserted a long strip of cardboard between the anode and cathode leads of the LEDs to avoid accidental short circuits.

❏ Now insert the two integrated circuits (ICs). They must not be reversed. The pin 1 connection on each is to be at lower left when viewed from the top of the board. The left side of the IC is the one with the indent marked into the plastic case. The 4017 IC is subject to static electricity damage and is supplied with its pins pushed into a pink or black foam strip. Remove this last before plugging in the IC. When the IC is in the circuit any danger of static kill is removed. The ICs may be a tight fit; spring them carefully into the sockets, being careful not to bend any pins.

The circuit will now operate. Power can come from a 9-volt battery because the current consumption is low, or you can use the power supply described in Chapter 3. The circuit will also operate from a 12-volt DC supply—increase R1 from 1k to 1.2 kilohms.

Although I've shown the LEDs in a line, there's no reason to keep them this way; they could be in a circle. If 3 mm lights are too big for your scale they can be mounted behind the walls with "viewing ports" of smaller diameter for the outside world.

Sequencing chase lights or traffic signals

The circuit illustrated in fig. 2-20 gives automatic switching of three lamps in sequence. Power transistors are included so up to 3 amps' worth of lamps can be switched—equivalent to 20 or 30 grain-of-wheat lamps. The advantage of this circuit over the circuit of fig. 2-13 is that the 10-milliamp current restriction is removed.

For chase lights, groups of lamps

Fig. 2-17. (Right) Top view of sequencer-traffic light board.

Fig. 2-18. (Far right) Printed circuit board layout (copper side, full size) for sequencer-traffic light board.

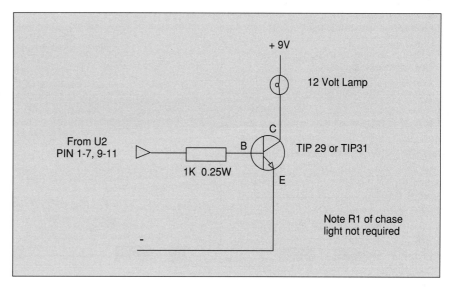

Fig. 2-16. Add to chase light (one per light) when using incandescent lamps. Any current of small lamp is okay.

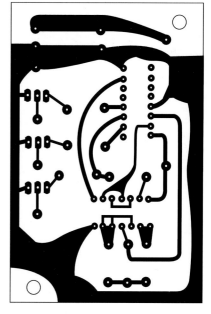

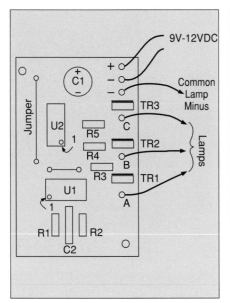

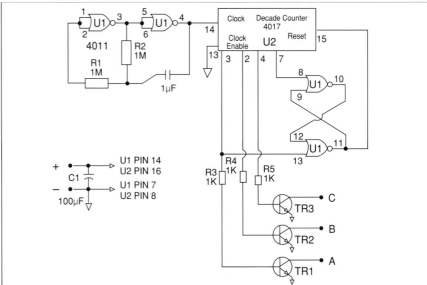

Fig. 2-19. (Above) Component locations for the sequencer-traffic light board.

Fig. 2-20. (Above right) Schematic of the sequencer-traffic light.

can be switched so that lines of lamps can be sequenced. By cross-connecting lamps in pairs you can make traffic signals. The traffic signals are not necessarily prototypical because the red, yellow, and green are on for equal times and the sequence is faster than in real life—but the accelerated lights look better on the model.

You'll need a printed circuit board, made as described in Chapter 1. Assembly steps are:

❏ Insert the 14-pin socket for U1 and the 16-pin socket for U2. Carefully solder the socket pins to the PC board. Don't solder pins that have no copper connection (there are several on U2). Insert the ICs last of all; keep them plugged into the conductive foam they came in until you are ready for them.

❏ Insert the five resistors and two capacitors. C1 is an electrolytic capacitor and must be inserted with the negative connection pointing down the board, as in the photograph. C2 can be connected either way.

❏ Insert the three TIP29 or TIP31 transistors. Their metal flanges go to the "up" side of the PC board, as shown in the photograph.

❏ Insert the two jumper wires—from pin 13 of U1 to pin 3 of U2, and from pin 16 of U2 to +.

❏ Connect two leads for the power supply, which can be a 9-volt battery for testing; for permanent installation see the 12-volt power supply in

PARTS LIST FOR TRAFFIC SIGNALS OR GROUP CHASE LIGHTS (FIG. 2-20)	
U1	Digital integrated circuit (CMOS) MC14001MCP: Digi-Key CD4001BCP; Mouser CD4001CBE
U2	Digital integrated circuit (CMOS) Mc14017BCP: Digi-Key CD4017BCN or MN4001B; Mouser CD4017BE
R1, R2	1-megohm, 0.25 watt resistors
R2, R3, R4	1K, 0.25-watt resistors
C1	100μF, 16-volt electrolytic capacitor
C2	Film or ceramic capacitor (not electrolytic), 0.22, 1, or 4.7μF, 25, 63, or 100 volt. (The cycle takes about 40 seconds with the larger value; it is faster with the lower capacitance value.)
TR1,2,3	TIP29 (for 1-amp switching) or TIP31 (up to 3-amp switching) transistors: Digi-Key TIP29PH-ND or TIP31PH-ND; Mouser 511-TIP29 or 511-TIP31
Miscellaneous	14- and 16-pin IC sockets PC board material On-off switch Wire

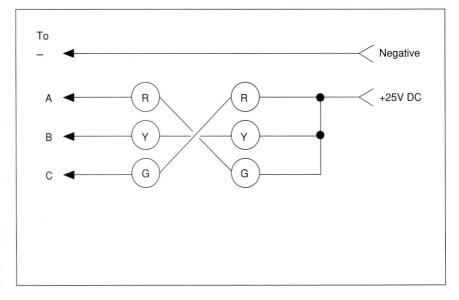

Fig. 2-21. Connecting opposing traffic lights to the sequencer circuit. Lamps are 12- to 16-volt incandescents. LEDs can be used if a 1.2K, 0.5-watt resistor is in series with the +25 volt DC supply.

Fig. 2-22. Connecting incandescents in a chase light. Bulbs 1, 4, and 7; 2, 5, and 8; and 3, 6, and 9 cycle on in sequence. Other triples can be added. Use 12-volt bulbs.

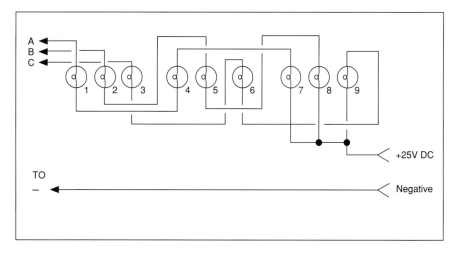

Chapter 3. Do not exceed 12 volts; the ICs are rated for 15 volts maximum.

❏ Connect leads A, B, and C, which go to the switched connections of the lamps, and connect the extra negative (-) connection for their return lead.

❏ Insert the two ICs, U1 and U2. They will be a tight fit because IC pins are slightly sprung into their sockets. Push them in firmly after ensuring there are no misaligned pins.

This completes the assembly. The power supply to the lamps can be the same 9-volt battery or 12-volt DC supply that powers the circuit, or it can be a separate source, but it must be filtered DC. I've shown an example in fig. 2-23 that uses a power pack as a source of 16 volts AC, which gives about 25 volts DC after it is rectified and filtered. Two or three 12-volt lamps can be switched in series by each transistor on the PC board.

I have a model of a CLRV (Canadian Light Rail Vehicle) to which I'd like to apply full exterior lighting, including stop lights and turn signals. How can I do it?

Fortunately this model is in O scale, giving enough space for the 18 lamps required: in front, two green classification lights, two amber turn signals, two white tracklamps, and a white headlight; rear, two red tail lights, two red stop lights, two amber turn signals, and two running lights (red); an amber turn signal on each side; and a blue light over the exit door. The turn signals are to operate but not flash. The stop lights and the blue door light are to turn on when the streetcar slows and turn off when it starts to move.

The particular model, one of a pair constructed by Neill Thornton of Scarborough, Ontario, Canada, is DC powered from the track and the overhead pole. A photo of one of Thornton's models is in fig. 2-25.

The diagram of fig. 2-24 shows how these components are wired. The headlamp and the track lights are 1.5-volt incandescent lamps connected across a bridge rectifier in series with one motor lead—a standard constant-lighting circuit. LEDs are used for the

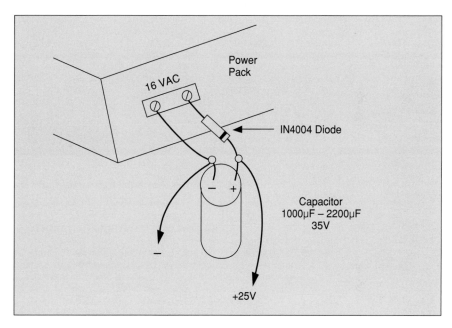

Fig. 2-23. Obtaining 25-volt filtered DC from the 16-volt fixed AC terminals of a power pack.

other lights. All 13 are powered from the 9-volt battery (fig. 2-24 does not include the two turn signal lights on the car sides). To keep current low, I specified high-efficiency 2-milliamp LEDs. The exception was the blue LED for the exit door, which runs at 18 milliamps. (High-efficiency blue LEDs hadn't been invented at time of the project!) The total LED current is no more than 45 milliamps, even when the turn signals are lit.

The brake lights and the blue door light are supplied through the battery and the relay contacts, but only when the relay is unpowered. That is when the track voltage falls below that required to energize the relay, as happens when the streetcar is almost

stopped. The relay stays unpowered until track voltage increases to send the car on its way. The coil is energized, the contacts open, and the blue and the red stoplights go out. All other lamps except the three white lights are on at all times, so there is a battery on-off switch.

The turn signals are controlled by a pair of small magnets and reed switches actuated when the front truck turns. The positioning may be awkward with some models, but the parts list indicates very small parts for these items. Self-flashing LEDs can be used for the turn signals. The yellow Marktech MT605FY operates on 9 volts, is 5 mm in diameter, and takes 38 milliamps for each lamp.

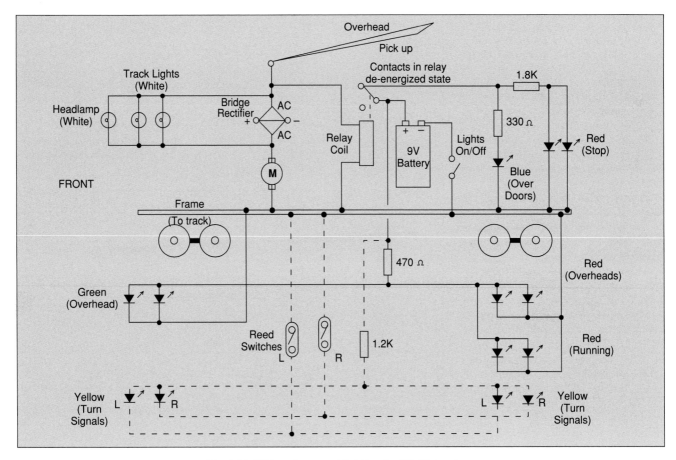

Fig. 2-24. Wiring of external lighting for CLRV streetcar.

PARTS LIST FOR STREETCAR LIGHTING	
Bridge rectifier	50-volt, 1.5-amp or greater: Radio Shack 276-1156
Front track lights	1.5-volt, 15-milliamp incandescents: Miniatronics
Headlamp	1.5-volt, 40- to 60-milliamp: Miniatronics
Relay	5- or 6-volt coil, SPDT contacts: Mouser 431-1206; Digi-Key 2773-ND; Omron G5V-1-DC5
Blue LED	Cree 101CR-ND: Digi-Key
Red LEDs	3mm: Quality Technologies Corp. HLMP-1700QT
Green LEDs	3mm: Quality Technologies Corp. HLMP-1790QT
Yellow LEDs	3mm: Quality Technologies Corp. HLMP-1719QT
Reed Switches	Newark Electronics 33F1067: Hamlin MINI-35-115
Magnets	Newark Electronics 33F1090: Hamlin H31-604; Radio Shack 64-1880 is larger (½" diameter)

How can fluorescent room lights be dimmed?

Variable dimming of the layout room lights contributes enormously to the effect of trains, locomotives, signals, and yard and building lights. Incandescent lights are no problem; rotary dimmers that replace the wall switch for incandescent lamps are common and cost only a few dollars. But many of us have twin 40-watt (4-foot) fluorescent lamp fixtures.

Just becoming available at time of writing are replacement electronic ballasts that are not only more efficient than the conventional ballasts used in these fixtures, but also are electronically dimmable. One such model is the Advance Transformer Co. RDC-2S40-TP. A remotely adjustable 0- to 10-volt signal controls brightness from 20 percent to 100 percent. An electrical contractor will have details. Other advantages of these electronic ballasts are quietness, efficiency, and long life; the disadvantage is cost. Replacement of a ballast in a fluorescent fixture should be undertaken only by professionals.

How can I model fluorescent building lights?

In one of the electronics magazines I found advertised a backlight for an Epson 2-inch screen TV receiver. The photo of fig. 2-26 shows the relative size with an HO station. These panels give a clear white light, much like a liquid crystal display and operate on 3 or 6 volts DC depending on size. Items such as this are not always available—watch the ads!

Tubular incandescent lamps are available, but because of the yellowish cast of the light they produce they are not as satisfactory as the electronic backlights. In his article "Modeling a Mood" in the January 1989 issue of

Fig. 2-25. Neill Thornton's abundantly lit O scale model of CLRV streetcar. Wiring was done by Thomas J. McConnell.

Fig. 2-26. Backlight panels from a miniature TV serve as building fluorescents. The station is HO scale.

Model Railroader, John Armstrong suggests that a way to reduce the yellowish cast of incandescent building lights is to paint all reflective surfaces pale blue.

3 Power supplies, switches, relays, and other components

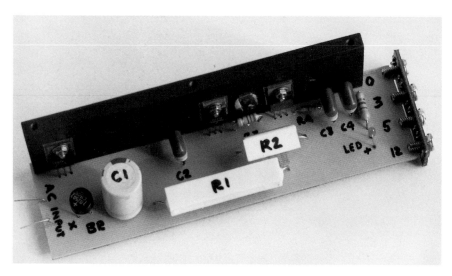

Fig. 3-1. Three-voltage power supply for bench use and testing.

PARTS LIST FOR POWER SUPPLY

R1	5-ohm, 10-watt resistor (for 16-volt AC input) or 1-ohm, 5-watt (for 12- or 12.6-volt AC input): Mouser 28PR010-5 or 28PR005-1.0; Digi-Key (Yageo) 5.0W-10 or 1.0W-5
R2	330-ohm, 0.25-watt resistor
R3	220-ohm, 0.25-watt resistor
R4	820-ohm, 0.25-watt resistor
TTR (12-volt)	7812 (generic); Mouser L78S12CV; Digi-Key (Panasonic) AN7812
TTR (5-volt)	7805 (generic); Mouser L7805CV; Digi-Key (Panasonic) AN7805
TTR (3-volt)	LM317 (generic); Mouser LM317T; Digi-Key (Samsung) LM317TKS
LED	Light-emitting diode, any source or type
C1	1,000µF, 25-volt electrolytic capacitor: Digi-Key (Panasonic) P6625; Mouser 140-XR25V1000
C2, C3, C4	Film capacitors, 0.22µF, 100-volt or higher: Mouser (Xicon) 140-PM2A224K; Digi-Key (Panasonic) P6625
BR1	Bridge rectifier, 1.5-amp, 100-PIV or higher: Digi-Key (G.I.) W01M; Mouser 333-B20S
Heat sinks	Use three rated at 10 or 11 degrees Celsius per watt (with 6-20 screws and nuts for mounting the TTRs: Mouser 567-7-320-BA or 33HS221 If a you use a common aluminum heat sink panel, you will need mica insulating washers, metal washers, insulating bushings and 6-20 screws and nuts: Radio Shack 276-1373
Power sources	16-volt AC, train power pack 12-volt AC, 1.5-amp wall transformer: Digi-Key T613-ND 12.6-volt AC, 2-amp transformer: Mouser (HiQ) 41LG015; also Radio Shack

A FAMILIARITY with the components is a necessary prelude to assembling them into throttle, signal, and sound circuits. It may help you to understand why your switch-machine pushbuttons melt in your hand—or to purchase block toggles that work well and feel right.

Is there a stable, short-circuit-proof power source for lamps and LEDs?

As you saw in the previous chapter, resistors can be used in series with lamps to allow the use of a power supply with voltage higher than the rating of the lamps. If you use as many lights as I do, though, it's convenient to have a power supply of the correct voltage. The circuit in fig. 3-1 gives 12 volts, 5 volts, and 3 volts at 1.5 amps total. You can draw 500 milliamps (0.5 amps) at each of three voltages or 1.5 amps at any one. The supply is also useful for testing or running-in locomotives, relays, switches, and LEDs before installation.

The power supply relies on three three-terminal regulators, which are integrated circuits in transistor cases. They accept higher DC voltage inputs and provide a fixed, stable DC output. They automatically shut themselves down if they overheat or if too much current is drawn through them. The input can be 12 volts AC from a wall-socket plug-in power supply, 12.6 volts from a separate 1.5- or 2-amp power transformer, or 16 volts AC from a train power pack.

After fabricating the printed circuit board (fig. 3-2), insert all the components except the three-terminal regulators (TTR). Resistors R1 and R2 are power resistors that afford a pre-drop of voltage, so the TTRs work more easily. They must be mounted with a little space between their lower surfaces and the PC board because they get warm. Watch the polarity on

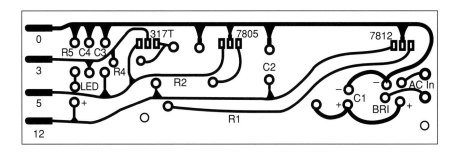

Fig. 3-2. PC board for three-voltage power supply (copper side, full size).

BR1, the bridge rectifier, and C1, the filter capacitor.

Next add the TTRs. The connections for these differ; the adjustable TTR used as the 3-volt source is the oddball. For the TTRs you can use separate heat sinks or a single one. No special insulation is required between the separate heat sinks and the TTRs. If you use a common cooling surface, as I did (a piece of scrap ⅛"-thick aluminum), insulating mica washers and insulating bushes are required because the metal backs of the TTRs are connected to one of the leads.

Finally, solder the set of four screw terminals to the copper pads on the underside of the PC board, and mark which terminal furnishes which voltage. As this is intended as a bench supply, there is no need to place it in an enclosure; but if you enclose it, provide some ventilation.

When you are testing locomotive motors, a TTR may shut itself off. Because the stall current of the motor is higher than the running current, the TTR sees the stall current as an overload. If this happens, place a 1- or 2-ohm resistor in series with one motor lead. Simple home-made throttles that use a TTR as the prime control device often have this problem; the solution is the same.

What are SMPSs?

The letters stand for switch mode power supply. They are usually manufacturers' surplus and are useful if the voltage, current, and price are right. Many components in these units work at 110 volts, so box them in carefully. The output is pure DC; pulse can't be added easily. The product should be UL tested for your reassurance. SMPS operate by semiconductor switching of the 60Hz AC line voltage to 50 to 100kHz or even higher. In consequence the transformer and filter capacitors are much smaller, in part

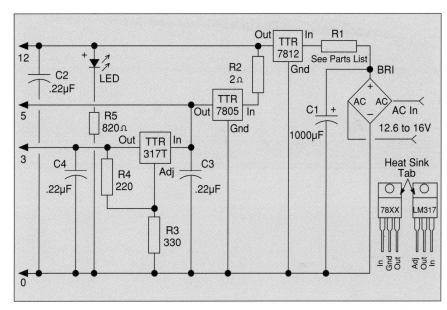

Fig. 3-3. Schematic for power supply.

Fig. 3-4. Toggle, rocker and slide switches offer similar functions yet quite different feel.

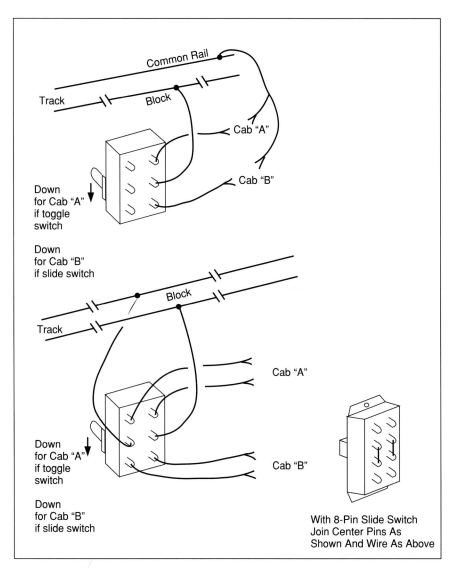

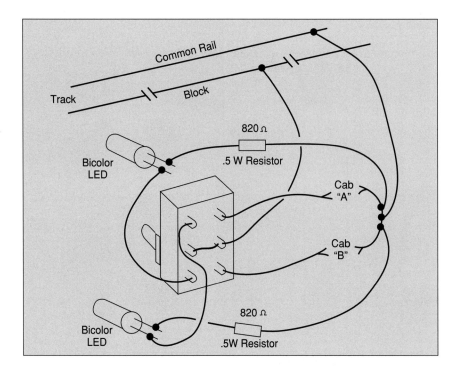

because the "gaps" between the AC pulses are much shorter and need less filtering to produce DC.

Can a car battery charger be used as a power source?

I do not recommend it. Some produce unfiltered pulsing DC, and others have an electronically regulated circuit that decreases output current as the load decreases. Both could cause problems. Most car battery chargers are high-current devices, and a short circuit could melt even Code 100 rail!

Test meters

A test meter capable of measuring AC and DC volts, DC current, and resistance is useful for monitoring track shorts and battery condition, as well as testing incandescent lamps and motor connections. I recommend an analog-scale multimeter (with a classic moving needle instead of a high-tech contemporary digital readout). Radio Shack carries these, often at special prices.

Block selector switches

A block is a section of track that is electrically isolated. A throttle, power pack, or cab is connected to the block through a block selector switch. The novice model railroader intuitively thinks of a block selector switch as a way to connect one throttle to several blocks, but the opposite is the case: a block selector switch connects any one of two or more throttles to one block. If you think of a block selector switch as a funnel or a trunk-and-branch system, the narrow end is at the track, not the throttle.

Start with the trivial case of one block and one throttle. Two wires connect the throttle to the track. Add a second throttle. You can remove the wires from the terminals of the first throttle and attach them to the second, but a switch makes the job easier. You have two wires, so you need a two-pole (or double-pole) switch; and two throttles, so it must be a two-throw (or double-throw) switch. On the

Fig. 3-6. Using spare pins on a center-off DPDT block switch to control LEDs. The bicolor LEDs indicate cab in use, direction, and voltage.

Fig. 3-7. Wiring center-off DPDT switches for direction or reversing-loop control. Cab and track pairs can be interchanged.

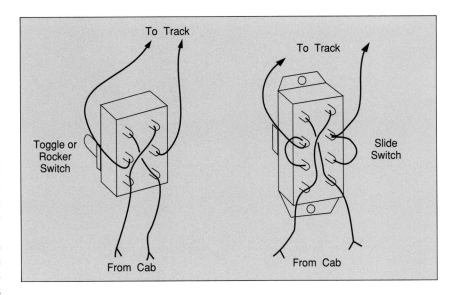

back of the typical double-pole, double-throw (DPDT) switch are six terminals, two at each end and two in the middle. Moving the lever of the switch one way connects the middle terminals to those at one end; moving it the other way, to the terminals at the other end. Many switches have a center-off position, at which the middle terminals are connected to neither end. See fig. 3-5.

If you use common-rail (common-return) wiring, you need use only one set of contacts on the double-pole, double-throw switch, leaving the other set of contacts free for a pair of LEDs indicating which throttle is connected to the block (fig. 3-6). Bicolor LEDs can indicate direction by color and track voltage by brightness. Another option with common-rail wiring is to use a less expensive single-pole, double-throw (SPDT) switch.

The LEDs can be Radio Shack 276-012, Dialight 521-9177, or IDI Devices 4301H1/S. They must be two-pin types, not three-pin.

Consider the touch and feel of the switches you choose. The center position of slide switches is often hard to find, and some small toggle switches are quite stiff. If you're ordering by mail, you may want to buy and test one switch before you order them by the dozen.

Is there a simple, foolproof reversing-loop circuit?

Reversing loops cause problems. They are the Möbius strips of model railroading. The right-hand rail, which is one polarity, twists around and runs into the left-hand rail, which is the opposite polarity; westbound trains become eastbounds without any action on the part of the direction switch.

A single pair of rail gaps halfway around the loop isn't enough. There must be two pairs of gaps creating an isolated section longer than the train, so there's no chance that metal wheels at opposite ends will bridge the gaps simultaneously.

To understand the other problem, you have to think about what the reversing switch on the throttle unit does (with conventional DC wiring). It doesn't make the locomotive move forward and backward but (to choose

arbitrary directions) east and west. If you pick up a westbound locomotive, turn it around, and set it back on the rails without touching the reversing switch, it will continue to move west. It will move east only when you change the polarity of the track with the reversing switch. A reversing loop requires an isolated section of track where the polarity can be held constant while the polarity of the main line is reversed.

Charles A. Harman's offered a solution in the December 1988 issue of *Model Railroader*, page 192. In fig. 3-9, a train entering the reversing loop along the straight (Block A) is automatically stopped at Block B when SPDT switch SW2 is in the position shown in the diagram. LP1 is a small incandescent lamp that offers enough resistance in series with the track power to stop the locomotive (Radio Shack 273-224 or any 12-volt, 40- to 60-milliamp lamp). With power on, it lights to advise you that the locomotive is standing in Block B, ready to re-enter the main. Throw the auxiliary reversing switch, SW1, and also SW2. If power is correct, the bicolor LED (Radio Shack 276-012) lights and the train moves into the main. If another LED-R1 combination is wired across Block A, the colors of the two LEDs will match, either red or green, if polarity is correct. Resistor R1 is 470 ohms, 0.5 watt. You must reset SW2 to the "stop-in-Block-B" position after train leaves. Block B can be about half again as long as the longest locomotive on your roster.

Switch wiring still looks complex.

Is there a simpler way?

Atlas offers several devices that simplify wiring of blocks and turnouts. They come with wiring diagrams and are ideal for beginners.

The 215 Selector has four SPDT center-off slide switches to control four blocks (215s can be ganged together in a matter of seconds). The 220 Controller accepts inputs from two cabs, has four DPDT center-off switches, and includes reversing loop or turntable polarity switching. It too can be ganged. The 205 Connector has three DPDT switches for auxiliary lighting on-off. (Like all other DPDT switches, these can be used as either single-pole or double-pole on-off switches.) Type 56 is a pushbutton turnout controller.

My switch-machine pushbuttons don't last long. Why?

A pushbutton is a momentary-action SPDT switch. Switch machine motors take a great deal of current in short bursts when they are triggered by the pushbutton. Peco and Atlas machines aren't too bad, but some heavy-duty twin-coil machines can draw up to 12 amps.

Radio Shack pushbutton 275-1547 is rated at 0.25 amp. Radio Shack 275-8077 and Mouser 10PA005 are rated at 3 amps. Digi-Key 502P is rated at 10 amps. The secret of long life is not using 0.25 amp pushbuttons on 12-amp switch machines!

Current ratings are often ignored in the hobby. If you are in the heavy-current brigade (O scale with Pittman motors, for example) you may want to check ratings on your reversing and

Fig. 3-8. Rolling stock with internal battery lighting or sound needs an unobtrusive switch to turn off the battery. This small C&K switch is shown with an HO scale caboose. It could be mounted under the floor.

designed for very low resistance in very-low-voltage circuits. If you've had problems with big motor systems, use switches specified for automotive applications. They are mostly rated at 10 to 20 amps.

I keep destroying the power transistor in my homemade walk-around throttles. It seems to happen when I throw the direction switch.

Chances are the DPDT direction switch was not a center-off type but a "make before break" type, in which the contacts for one direction are open only after the contacts for the reverse direction are closed. This means that a short circuit appears across the throttle output every time the direction switch is operated, and if the reversal occurs at full speed (heaven forbid!) the transistor gets recurring heavy

block switches. Two identical-looking switches may have a large difference in ratings. The C&K E010 series of push buttons, for example, is rated at either 0.25 amp or 4 amps. The internal difference is that the lower-rated contacts are gold plated; they're

Fig. 3-9. A reversing loop cannot avoid switches, even with command control. LEDs provide operator information.

PART NUMBERS FOR SWITCHES

There are some sixty makers of switches in the U.S. Many have direct substitutes for the numbers shown below.

Toggle switches

SPDT center off	Digi-Key CKN1004-ND (small)
	C&K 7101SYCQE (small)
DPDT center off	Digi-Key CKN1001-ND
	C&K 7201SYCQE
3 pole center off	Digi-Key CKN1037-ND
	C&K 7301SYZQE

Rocker switches

SPDT center off	Digi-Key CKN2002-ND
	C&K U11J51ZQE22
	Digi-Key SW305-ND (black)
	C W Ind. GRS-4013A-1300 (black)
	Digi-Key SW306-ND (red)
	C W Ind. GRS-4013A-0008 (red)
DPDT center off	Digi-Key SW309-ND (black)
	C W Ind. GRS-4023A-1300 (black)
	Digi-Key SW310-ND (red)
	C W Ind. GRS-4023A-0009 (red)

These rocker switches fit into panels up to 0.18" thick.

Slide switches

2-pole, 3-position	Digi-Key SW107-ND; C W Ind. G1128S-1110
4-pole, 3-position	Digi-Key SW108-ND; C W Ind. G660S-6010
SPDT center off	Radio Shack 275-8011
DPDT center off	Radio Shack 275-510

jolts of current. Choose a center-off or "break before make" switch. If you use rotary block-selector switches (most of them are rated only for low currents) use non-shorting ones, not the kind with shorting contacts.

I need a tiny on-off switch for battery-powered lights in passenger cars and cabooses.

The photo of fig. 3-8 shows a "surface mount" switch and a small LED on the roof of an HO caboose. This type of switch can be fitted to a car floor in almost any scale with epoxy or cyanoacrylate adhesive. The switch shown is a C&K GT01, a SPDT type rated at 250 milliamps at 12 volts. Surface mount components are usually the smallest available in any category, but they require careful soldering.

What are reed switches?

Reed switches are magnetically triggered contacts sealed in a small glass tube. For model railroad use they are usually mounted between the rails. A magnet under the locomotive turns the switch on as it passes over the reed switch. Reed switches are useful for track detection and signaling systems that are completely independent of track power.

Where can I get reed switches?

Hamlin Inc. supplied the reeds and magnets for the streetcar direction lights described in Chapter 1. Hamlin MDRR-4-104 is a 1 Form A (SPST) type, 0.60" long and 0.105" in diameter. The magnet is Hamlin H-33, which is a bar magnet, 0.75" long with 0.12" edges. The switch is rated at 0.5 amp up to 20 volts.

When a coil is wound around a reed switch so the switch forms the core of an electromagnet, the device is termed a reed relay. These are widely used in home security systems, but in general are too large for model railroad use.

Relays

Relays are magnetically operated switches. A coil of copper wire with a soft iron core acts as an electromagnet, which pulls an armature to operate one or more switches with anywhere from two to ten contacts. Relays have the advantage that a small current in the coil can control circuits carrying lots of amps, and those circuits can be

Fig. 3-10. Typical small relays used in model railroads. Some of these are as small as integrated circuits yet can switch amps of current with a life of a million operations.

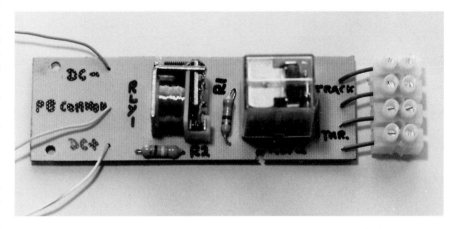

Fig. 3-11. This relay reverser offers memory and remote pushbutton control of locomotive direction.

completely isolated from the coil. The ignition key in your car is a switch that controls a relay. The relay contacts control the 150-amp current of the starter motor. Fortunately, model railroading has not yet reached such current levels—not even G scale!

You'd expect relays to be labeled SPST, DPDT, since they are switches (some catalogs list them that way), but the manufacturers use a different code. A "1 Form A" contact is SPST; a "1 Form C" is a SPDT; "2 Form C" is DPDT; "4 Form C" is four-pole, double-throw. Form K denotes center-off relay contacts. Avoid "make before break" contacts if you use the relay to reverse train direction.

Relays are reliable. Typical guar-anteed life is a million cycles for the mechanical parts of the relay and 200,000 cycles for the contacts at full ratings.

The main use of relays is for signals; they are also used as an interface between low-current track detection circuits such as the Twin-T and higher powered crossing gates, flashers, sound systems, and the like. They have an advantage over integrated circuits in being easier to understand and troubleshoot. If the relay clicks when it should, then all the preceding circuitry is good!

Reversing relay for a walkaround throttle

A walkaround throttle of the type

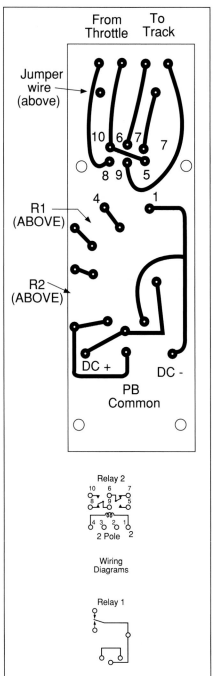

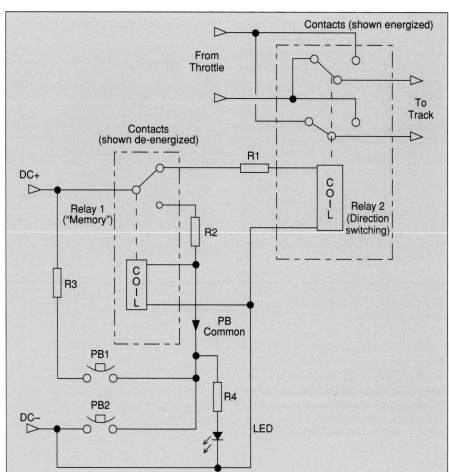

Fig. 3-12. (Above) PC board layout for reverser (copper side, full size). For different relays, you may need to change the layout.

Fig. 3-13. (Above right) Schematic of reverser. For values see the parts list. Not all components shown are on the PC board.

PARTS LIST FOR REVERSER (FIG. 3-13)

Relay 1	SPDT (1 Form C), 1 amp or more: Potter & Brumfield T90N5D12-12 (Newark Electronics 90F1125) for N, HO, and O scales (12-volt coil) Potter & Brumfield T90N5D12-24 (Newark 90F1126) for G scale (24-volt coil)
Relay 2	DPDT (2 Form C), 5 amp: Potter & Brumfield R10-E2-X2-V185 (Newark 46F3505) for N, HO, and O scales (12-volt coil) Potter & Brumfield R10-E2-X2-V700 (Newark 67F1078) for G scale (24-volt coil)
R1	33-ohm, 0.5 watt resistor if you use the Relay 2 specified above for N, HO, and O; otherwise a resistor of about 25 percent of the resistance of the Relay 2 coil R1 is not required if you use 24-volt relays
R2, R3	39-ohm, 0.5-watt resistor if you use the Relay 1 specified above for N, HO, and O; otherwise a resistor of about 25 percent of the resistance of the Relay 1 coil 22-ohm, 0.5-watt resistor for G scale
R4	680-ohm, 0.5 watt resistor for N, HO, and O scales; 820-ohm, 0.5 watt resistor for LGB
Miscellaneous	PCB material, 4.25" × 1.375" Different voltage relays and resistors are specified for LGB because the throttle-filtered DC voltage is nominally 12 to 14 volts for the smaller gauges. LGB throttles usually are 17 to 21 volts. The DC source for the reverser is this DC voltage.

that lets you unplug the control head and plug it in elsewhere while the train maintains speed requires a reverser with memory. Relays are ideal for this function. Although there are latching relays with ratchets that alternate contacts with each operation, they are expensive and hard to get. (The reverser in Lionel locomotives is driven by a latching relay. As the throttle is opened, the coil is energized, changing the contacts so the

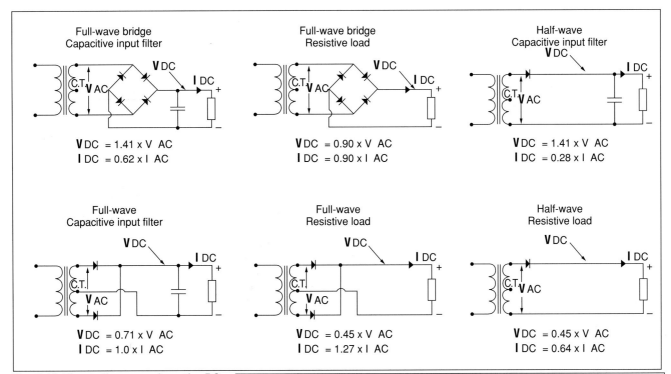

Full-wave bridge
Capacitive input filter

$$V_{DC} = 1.41 \times V_{AC}$$
$$I_{DC} = 0.62 \times I_{AC}$$

Full-wave bridge
Resistive load

$$V_{DC} = 0.90 \times V_{AC}$$
$$I_{DC} = 0.90 \times I_{AC}$$

Half-wave
Capacitive input filter

$$V_{DC} = 1.41 \times V_{AC}$$
$$I_{DC} = 0.28 \times I_{AC}$$

Full-wave
Capacitive input filter

$$V_{DC} = 0.71 \times V_{AC}$$
$$I_{DC} = 1.0 \times I_{AC}$$

Full-wave
Resistive load

$$V_{DC} = 0.45 \times V_{AC}$$
$$I_{DC} = 1.27 \times I_{AC}$$

Half-wave
Resistive load

$$V_{DC} = 0.45 \times V_{AC}$$
$$I_{DC} = 0.64 \times I_{AC}$$

Fig. 3-14. These diagrams show the DC output voltages available from different combinations of transformers, rectifiers, and filters. Knowing your DC voltage and current requirement will help you specify the transformer.

field connections to the AC motor are reversed.) Latching relays draw a heavy current, often as much as the locomotive motor itself.

The circuit in fig. 3-13 uses two conventional low-current relays for direction control. Relay 2, which has 2 Form C (DPDT) contacts, is the main reversing relay. The coil of Relay 2 is energized only when Relay 1 is de-energized. Relay 1 has 1 Form C (SPDT) contacts that supply power to the coil of Relay 2 coil or to R2, R4, and the LED. PB1 and PB2 can be in a separate unit, with wire leads as long as necessary or convenient.

Pushbuttons PB1 and PB2, R3, R4, and the LED are in the control head along with the speed control (not shown). Only four wires are needed: DC positive, DC negative, the common lead of PB1 and PB2, and the slider of the speed-control potentiometer. For details on how this type of memory control is used with a transistor throttle, see Chapter 4.

When the throttle is first switched on, the fixed DC voltage energizes Relay 2 via R1. (R1 is needed only to reduce the voltage to Relay 2 if the DC voltage exceeds the relay rating by a significant amount.) Train direction at

TRANSFORMER SOURCES AND PART NUMBERS

Mouser Electronics	10-volt (CT), 2-amp	41LF020
	12.6-volt (CT), 1.5-amp	41LG015
	12.6-volt (CT), 3.0-amp	41LG030
	18-volt (CT), 1.5-amp	41LJ015
	18-volt (CT), 2.0-amp	41FJ020
Radio Shack	12.6-volt (CT), 1-amp	273-1505
	12.6-volt (CT), 3-amp	273-1511
	18-volt (CT), 2-amp	273-1515
Hammond Electronics	8.5-volt, 2-amp	166L8
	9-volt, 0.5-amp	166G9
	12.6-volt (CT), 4-amps	166N12
	16-volt (CT), 2.2-amps	166L12

All the above are for chassis mounting and have flexible color-coded connection wires. Don't overlook wall-mount plug-in power units for AC outputs; they are limited to the low currents.

RELAY SOURCES

1 Form C (SPDT)	Radio Shack 275-241, microminiature, 12-volt, 1-amp
	Mouser 433-743H, miniature, 12-volt, 10-amp
	Mouser 431-1305, miniature, 12-volt, 2-amp
	Digi-Key (Omron) G5LE-114P-PS-DC12, miniature, 12-volt, 10-amp
	Digi-Key (Omron) G5LE-114P-PS-DC24, miniature, 24-volt, 10-amp
2 Form C (DPDT)	Mouser 433-2411, miniature, 12-volt, 5-amp
	Mouser 431-OVR-SH-212L, 16-pin DIP, 12-volt, 1-amp
	Mouser 431-OVR-SH-224L, 16-pin DIP, 24-volt, 1-amp
	Digi-Key (Omron) G5V-2-H-DC12, 16-pin DIP, 12-volt, 2-amp
	Digi-Key (Omron) G5V-2-H-DC24, 16-pin DIP, 24-volt, 2-amp
	Potter & Brumfield R10-R2X2-V185, PC mount case, 12-volt, 5-amp
	Potter & Brumfield R10-R2X2-V700, PC mount case, 24-volt, 5-amp
4 Form C (4PDT)	Digi-Key (Omron) G6A-434P-ST-US-DC12, 16-pin DIP 12-volt, 1-amp
	Takamisawa MAT4B-BL, miniature 12-volt, 1-amp
	Takamisawa MAT4B-CL, miniature 24-volt, 1-amp
	Potter & Brumfield R10-2X4-V185, PC mount case, 12-volt, 5-amp
	Potter & Brumfield R10-2X4-V700, PC mount case, 24-volt, 5-amp
Suppliers	Potter & Brumfield relays are available from Newark Electronics, Mouser, and Digi-Key. Takamisawa relays are available from ITT Components.

The 16-pin DIP package is similar to an integrated circuit package in size and height.

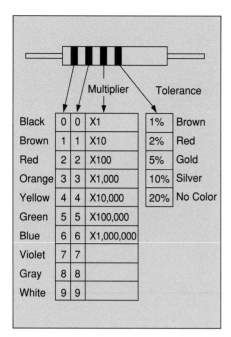

				Multiplier		Tolerance	
Black	0	0	X1		1%	Brown	
Brown	1	1	X10		2%	Red	
Red	2	2	X100		5%	Gold	
Orange	3	3	X1,000		10%	Silver	
Yellow	4	4	X10,000		20%	No Color	
Green	5	5	X100,000				
Blue	6	6	X1,000,000				
Violet	7	7					
Gray	8	8					
White	9	9					

Fig. 3-15. Resistor color code.

that point is forward. Pushing PB1 energizes the coil of Relay 1, whose SPDT contacts switch off Relay 2 and keep Relay 1 energized via R2, even when PB1 is released. R2 performs a similar function to R1, but also limits the current flowing in PB2 when PB2 is operated. The train direction is now reversed and stays that way, even if the control head is unplugged. Pushing PB2 shorts out the coil of Relay 1, which de-energizes, letting Relay 2 energize to the forward position again. (The pushbuttons do nothing when the control head is unplugged, of course.)

When the control head is plugged in, the LED lights up to indicate reverse. Resistor R4 limits the current in the LED. Resistor R3 is protection from shorting the DC positive to negative if PB1 and PB2 are pressed simultaneously.

The printed circuit layout for the reverser is in fig. 3-12. It applies to the relays specified in the parts list. If you use other relays, the layout will need rearranging. I recommend a minimum rating of 2 amps for Relay 2; 0.5 amp is sufficient for Relay 1.

Can the reverser be used for other applications or with other relays?

The reverser needs only one extra wire in a memory walkaround control cable. If you use an 8-wire cable, for example, you can control five motor-drive turnouts at each plug-in position as you walk around the layout, and

they remain in the set position when you replug into the next section and control another five. Five more LEDs in the control head would give you readouts of their positions.

Another possible function is a motor-controlled crossing gate that you could raise and lower directly from the walkaround control head as you proceed around the layout.

How critical is the relay coil voltage? Must it match the DC supply?

A typical relay specification covers maximum overvoltage, minimum dropout voltage, and maximum pull-in (pickup) voltage. For example, a 12-volt relay may have a maximum operating voltage of 18; pick up (operate) at 9 volts, and not drop out (de-energize) above 1.2 volts. The voltage tolerance of the relays specified in this book is wide enough to cover most model railroad conditions.

Transformers

Transformers isolate the line current and lower its voltage. The usual transformer is of a chunky rectangular shape; the low-profile but more expensive toroidal (doughnut-shaped) transformer is useful where space is tight.

Transformers are rated according to the power of the secondary coil. The figure is usually quoted in "VA," which is the same as watts for our purposes. A power pack rated at 15VA with a 12-volt output has a current rating of 1.25 amps (volts times amps equals watts). The ratings of most power packs are a total figure including DC for the trains and AC for the accessories.

Of what use is the center tap on many replacement transformers?

The center tap was used more often back when rectifiers were expensive devices made of selenium. The center tap allowed two rectifiers to do the job of four. Most packs today use an untapped transformer and four silicon diodes that are cheaper and more efficient. Fig. 3-14 shows different arrangements of tapped and untapped transformers and different numbers of diodes and the relationships between AC and DC voltages and currents. A center-tapped transformer plus two diodes may be cheaper than a non-center-tapped transformer plus four diodes. Filtered DC output has a higher voltage than the AC input;

pulsed DC, lower.

Is 25 volts DC from 16 volts AC a case of getting something for nothing?

No such luck. There's no perpetual motion machine for model railroaders! The power available is the limiting factor, and power is the product of volts and amps. If the voltage is higher, the current is lower.

How do I know what transformer I need?

Let's start with a transformer as input for a transistor throttle. You'll want a transformer with an output voltage equal to 70 percent of the full-speed voltage of your largest locomotives plus 2 volts for losses in the rectifier diodes and the transistors. Amperage rating should be at least 160 percent of the current draw of the largest locomotive; double that if you plan to doublehead. This formula assumes the power supply includes a full-wave bridge rectifier and capacitive input filter.

For Z scale you'll need an 8.4-volt transformer (70 percent of 12 volts); the nearest available size is 9 volts. If you need 1 amp of DC for the locomotives, the transformer should be at least 1.25 amps—more if it will also power lights and other accessories. For N scale you'll need a 12.6-volt transformer with a current rating of at least 2.4 amps. For HO and O you also need a 12.6 volt-transformer; minimum current ratings are 3.2 amps for HO and 4.8 amps for O. For G and larger you should have a 14- or 15-volt, 3.2-amp transformer.

The voltage is for the full secondary of the transformer; the center tap (if there is one) is not used. The current specified is higher than most commercial throttles would use. You can get away with a lower current rating, but the output voltage at full load will drop below the rated figure. This is not usually much of a problem. All transformers put out somewhat less than rated voltage at full load. The smaller the transformer, the greater the resistance and consequently the greater the voltage drop.

If the transformer is intended for powering incandescent lights, the current rating should be equal to the total current of all the lights. There's no problem if the transformer is rated for too much current. The voltage should match that of the lamps or be slightly less. Lamps last much longer if they receive slightly less than their full rated voltage.

A power supply for twin-coil switch machines requires a 12.6-volt transformer with a current rating of at least 3 amps. If you use a capacitive discharge circuit for the switch machines, you can use a smaller transformer. For motor-drive switch machines follow the manufacturer's recommendations.

Capacitors

Capacitors are two-wire components of two types, electrolytic and film. The latter category includes Mylar, foil, polyester, and paper.

Electrolytic capacitors are used as filters in power supplies and transistor throttles. They shunt or bypass residual AC so the DC is reasonably clean. They're also used as momentum capacitors in throttles. Electrolytics are polarized; their positive and negative terminals must be connected correctly. They have a molecular-thin separation layer between the conductive foil surfaces; the separation layer is formed as a chemical when the capacitor is charged. The thinness is the reason electrolytics have such a large capacity in a small volume. Electrolytic capacitors specified in this book range from 220 to 4,700 µF (microfarads).

Can you explain film capacitor markings?

Film capacitors range from 0.001 to 0.47 microfarad and can be connected in either direction. Some are marked with the value in microfarads. There may be a letter J or K, which indicates tolerance of 5 percent or 10 percent, respectively. Often the value is printed on the capacitor in picofarads (but without specifying the unit). There are a million picofarads in a microfarad. To add to the confusion the number of zeros in the value is assigned a number as the last digit. For example. A capacitor coded 474 is 47 plus four zeros—470,000 picofarads or 0.47 microfarad. The test meters we use can't measure capacitors.

What ripple current and temperature rating do I need?

Large electrolytics aren't specified just by capacity and voltage but also by ripple current and temperature. If your component source requires that you specify the ripple current, ask for at least double the DC current of the throttle or power supply. If you must specify temperature, an 85° C. rating is adequate, and the device will cost less than one with a 105° C. rating.

If you find that a filter capacitor gets warm in use, replace it with the next higher voltage rating.

Similar reasoning applies to the temperature rating. When they are used as filter they pass heavy AC loads and can get warm. (If they are wired in backward, they get so hot they pop off like a Roman candle!)

Most electrolytics are marked either for 85° or 105° (Celsius). In general the 105° capacitor will have the higher current rating and will cost more.

For use in other parts of throttles or power supplies, ripple current and temperature ratings do not affect us.

What about radial and axial leads?

Axial leads exit from opposite ends of the capacitor and are convenient for hand wiring. Radial leads emerge from the same end, making a more compact unit for printed circuit assembly. Radials generally cost less than axials.

Resistors

Resistors are the other two-lead passive component we use. They are rated in ohms, kilohms (thousands of ohms), and megohms (millions of ohms). The ratings are color-coded on small resistors—see fig. 3-15. In addition, our test meters can measure resistance. Resistors are also specified by wattage. Most that we use are 0.25- or 0.5-watt. Larger resistors have their ohm and watt ratings marked on them. In general, the higher the wattage, the bigger the resistor.

Older throttles generally use a rheostat, a variable resistor, as a speed control. Most of them can dissipate 25 or 50 watts of heat. The speed control in a transistor throttle is also a variable resistor or a potentiometer, but it has a much higher resistance than the older rheostat and needs to be rated only 0.5 watt.

4 Throttles, Power Packs, Cabs, and Speed Controls

MODEL TRAINS are propelled by electric motors. They need some kind of speed control. Whether you call it a throttle, a power pack, a cab, or simply a speed control is immaterial. They are all electrical or electronic devices that control the speed of the train. Some speed controls are better than others, but even the simplest power pack can be improved with simple electronics. The first project in this chapter shows how.

The chapter also includes an update of a popular throttle described in *Model Railroader* some time ago. This unit can be used as a walkaround control, attached to the layout with a flexible cable so you can follow the train close up. There's also another walkaround control that eliminates power current flowing in the remote cables and is suitable for G scale as well as HO and O. Another cab design has memory walkaround control.

Unlike the two previously described, which must be plugged in at all times, this push-button, cable-connected cab can be unplugged for 15 to 20 minutes while the train continues to run untended.

For those who are interested in the subtleties of braking, I've included a brake stand simulator (an update of a previous design) that enables a transistor throttle to have the added effect of true prototype simulation.

I use rheostat controls on my layout, but I can't make my newer locomotives stop. Why?

A rheostat is a variable resistor in series with the locomotive motor. Minimum resistance gives maximum speed and vice versa. Typical rheostats for model railroads have a maximum resistance of about 100 ohms. If you try to use a rheostat with one of today's efficient motors, which draws,

let's say, 370 milliamps at 12 volts (its resistance therefore is 33 ohms) the voltage across the motor at minimum speed can never be less than 33 divided by 133 times 12 volts, or about 3 volts. At 3 volts many motors are still turning. The more efficient the motor, the greater the voltage across it at what should be the stop position on the rheostat. You could solve the problem by connecting a 20-ohm, 5-watt resistor across the output, which would cut voltage across the motor to 2 volts at the stop position, but the real answer is to use transistors.

Can a rheostat power pack be converted to a transistor throttle?

Figs. 4-1 through 4-7 show the conversion of a Model Rectifier Corporation UC2001 dual-power throttle pack to transistor operation. The circuit is suitable for almost any unit up to 2 amps output. The modification lets

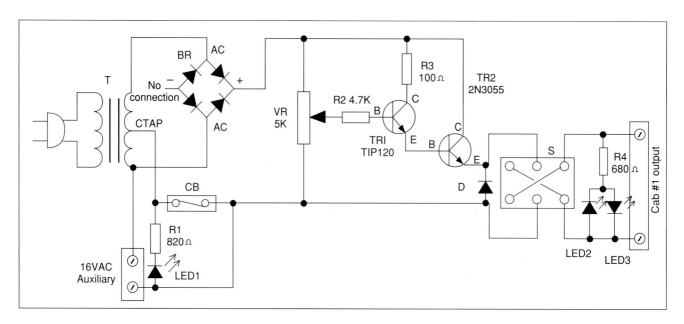

Fig. 4-1. Conversion of plain old power pack to transistor throttle. All 110-volt AC and switch wiring is unchanged.

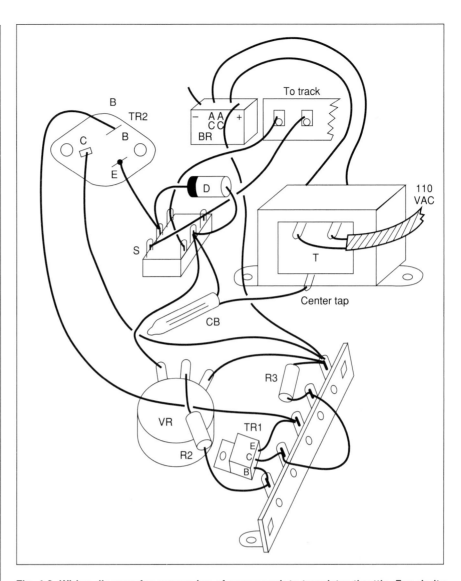

Fig. 4-2. Wiring diagram for conversion of power pack to transistor throttle. For clarity the optional LEDs and associated resistors are not shown.

you control even low-current can motors and eliminates jerky starts.

What causes jerky starts?

Starting practically anything requires more energy than keeping it going, and DC motors follow that rule. The current drops off the moment the motor starts turning, which means the voltage jumps up; so if you are using a variable resistor to control the motor speed, you have to adjust the resistance the moment the motor starts. For example, a Maxor high-efficiency 12-volt, 3-watt DC motor has a starting current of 231 milliamps and a no-load current of 13.5 milliamps. A transistor circuit is unaffected by the wide difference between starting and

Fig. 4-3. The power pack before conversion.

Fig. 4-4. The power pack after conversion to transistor controls.

Fig. 4-5. Interior of power pack before conversion. Switches and transformer wiring are not changed.

running motor current as it regulates the voltage to the motor.

Replacing rheostats with transistor circuits

Start by opening up the power pack (be sure it's unplugged) and discarding some of the innards. Retain the transformer, power cord, enclosure, on-off switch, direction switch, and short-circuit protection device. There may be more than one of some of these. Discard the rectifiers, which are usually selenium plates. They are obsolete and often a source of trouble. Also dump the rheostats—and the control knobs for the sake of appearance.

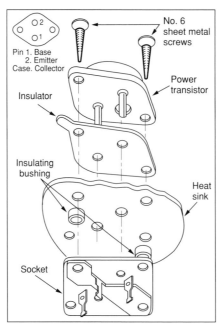

Fig. 4-6. Interior of power pack after transistor conversion. New speed control, two transistors, and terminal strip with components are added.

The transformer center tap goes to the glass overload device and remains so connected. The two other secondary wires go to the rectifiers on the back panel, which are replaced by silicon bridge rectifiers. The secondary wires go to the two connections marked AC.

The + connection of the bridge rectifier runs to the five-position terminal strip. The negative connection of the bridge is not used. The effect is to turn the bridge into a package containing just two diodes. It makes wiring easier because the diodes are in a package and not two free-standing items to be supported and soldered. Secure the bridge rectifier and the terminal strip

Fig. 4-7. Mounting TR2 to heat sink. Note the insulating bushings are part of the socket if you use the Keystone part in the list.

to the chassis with epoxy or gap-filling cyanoacrylate adhesive. I covered the bridge rectifier connections and the 110-volt transformer primary connections with an insulating compound (silicone sealant will do). Although this now obsolete power pack originally had safety approvals, exposed terminals are no longer acceptable.

To add LEDs to show overload and direction, follow the wiring diagram in fig. 4-2 and the photo of fig. 4-6. The LEDs are omitted from fig. 4-2 for clarity.

Connect TR1 and TR2 carefully. The metal side of the case faces down for TR1 and must not touch any metal. The pins of TR2 are located off center, towards the right in fig. 4-6. The case of TR2 is the C connection and must be insulated from the heat sink and the chassis (fig. 4-7) by using a socket, insulating washer, bushings, and thermal grease. There isn't room inside the power pack for TR2, so it is mounted outside. External mounting provides better cooling, too. You will likely have to cut away part of the power pack case so it fits over and around the heat sink.

The power pack had two auxiliary circuits: fixed-voltage DC from one the positive terminal of one rectifier and the center tap of the associated transformer, and fixed-voltage AC from the secondary of the other transformer. Both these circuits can be retained.

This circuit offers low resistance at all voltages, unlike the rheostat, which varies depending on the speed setting. The wave form of the output is unchanged—a 120-Hertz pulsating DC, a relatively smooth pulse that has little or no extra heating effect on motors. The design retains one limiting effect on performance, the resistance of the transformer. The one illustrated has a resistance of about 2 ohms. For a 1-amp current, the voltage to the transistors—and thus the track voltage—will drop by 2 volts, hardly noticeable for most motors.

Troubleshooting and testing

The circuit is rugged, and the transistors are rated much higher than required. (A few years ago this cost money, but nowadays we're talking nickels and dimes.) With a DC meter, check for 15 to 20 volts between the + lead of the bridge rectifier and negative side of the circuit. If there is no voltage, check for 16 to 18 volts AC between each AC connection of the bridge rectifier and the transformer center tap. If you get nothing there, the transformer, the power cord, or the on-off switch is defective. Be careful where you poke the leads of your test meter, because 110-volt AC is present in the primary side of the transformer.

As the speed control is turned, the DC voltage between the slider and the negative side of the circuit will swing from zero to 15 volts or so. The B (base) connection of TR1 will track this, as will the B and E (emitter) connections of TR2. Any break in this pattern means the preceding component could be defective, assuming all wiring is correct and the solder connections are good.

Some time back *Model Railroader* published a circuit for "the simplest transistor throttle." Is there an update for that?

Over the past twenty years, semiconductors have dropped drastically in price. The original design was very cost-conscious, and many model railroaders built it as their first electronic project. Fig. 4-9 shows one form of the original design. Though it was not specifically intended to be a tethered walkaround cab, most people built it as one. It's still a good first project; the improved and updated version shown in fig. 4-10 offers more power and flexibility than the original.

The 2ST—Second Simple Throttle

The 2ST has three components: power source, 16 to 18 volts AC at up to 3 amps; a rectifier and distribution unit located at the layout; and a control head with a long cord that plugs

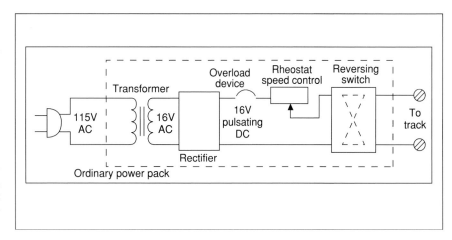

Fig. 4-8. A rheostat speed control cannot give smooth loco starts, though special tapered winding of the resistance wire on the rheostat helps.

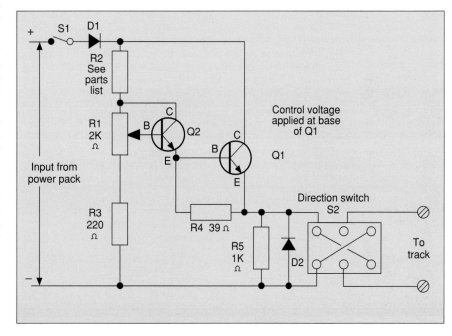

Fig. 4-9. Schematic of the original 1ST—the simplest transistor throttle.

into the rectifier-distribution unit. Train current flows through the cord, so it should be low resistance. For this reason I ruled out telephone cords and connectors and specified a DIN 5-conductor cord and connector, which can carry up to 4 amps. (Only four wires of the cable are used.)

Figs. 4-13 and 4-14 show the wiring of the two units. The components are few in number, so there is no merit in using a printed circuit. Item F is an overload protector, connected between the transformer and BR, the bridge rectifier. In this project, unlike the rheostat conversion above, all four connections of BR are used. This enables 2ST to have nearly twice

the output voltage of the original circuit, which had just a single diode rectifier.

The control head circuit is similar to the rheostat conversion circuit, but a larger heat sink is specified for TR2, permitting outputs up to 3 amps. The heat sink will get quite warm at high currents, particularly at medium speeds. It stays quite cool even with double-headed can-motored Atlas HO locomotives, but don't be surprised at heat with larger motors. It's normal and doesn't mean disaster is about to strike.

Diode D protects the circuit if another power supply is accidentally connected to the same block. It's not

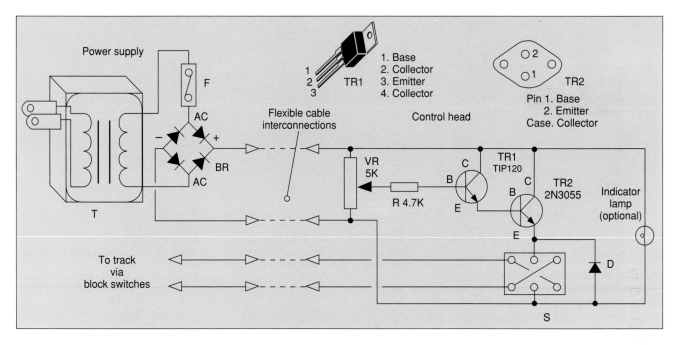

Fig. 4-10. Update for the simplest transistor throttle. With appropriate connecting cable this can be a tethered walkaround cab suitable for Z, N, and HO scales.

PARTS LIST FOR 2ST THROTTLE (FIG. 4-10)	
T	You have several choices: AC auxiliary connections of a power pack (25 VA minimum) Spare Lionel or American Flyer AC power pack Wall transformer, 16.5 volts, 1 amp: Jerome Industries PITB-113 Separate transformer: Mouser (HiQ) 41LJ015 (18 volts, 1.5 amps); Hammond 166 L16 (17 volts, 2.2 amps)—don't use the center tap on either
F	Automatic resetting overload protector Glass type, as used in most commercial packs: Hold 1 amp, trip at 2 amps, ECG202 or MB-315 (Philips ECG) Hold 2 amp, trip at 4 amps, ECG204 or MB-316 (Philips ECG) Solid state type Polyswitch Hold 1.1 amp, trip 2.13 amps, RBE110A (available from Raychem) Hold 2.05 amp, trip 3.77 amps, RBE205A (available from Raychem)
BR	Bridge rectifier, minimum 100 volts and 3 amps: Digi-Key GBPC602; Mouser 333-BR32
TR1	TIP120 NPN Darlington transistor: Mouser 511-TIP120; Digi-Key TIP120GE-ND; Jameco 32993
TR2	2N3055 NPN transistor: Mouser 511-2N3055; Radio Shack 276-2041; Jameco 38308
D	100-volt, 3-amp diode: Digi-Key 1N5401; Mouser 333-RL252; Radio Shack 266-1154; Jameco 36249
VR	5,000-ohm, 0.5-watt, linear-taper rotary potentiometer: Mouser 31VA305; Radio Shack 271-1714; Jameco 29196
DIN cable	5-pin type, with plug at one or both ends: Mouser 172-5910; a computer keyboard cable is suitable, as in fig. 4-4: Jameco 22234
DIN socket	5-pin type, chassis mount: Digi-Key (Cui Stack) CP-1250-ND; Radio Shack 274-005; Jameco 15843
S	Double-pole, center off switch—see Chapter 2 for parts selection
R	4.7K, 0.25-watt resistor
Utility cases	Control head—plastic, may have aluminum panel, approximately 5" × 2.5" ×.5": Radio Shack 270-233; Digi-Key SR033-ND; Hammond 1591CSBK. Rectifier-distribution unit—plastic, approximately 3" × 2" × 1.5": Radio Shack 270-230; Digi-Key L111-ND; Hammond 1591LSBK
Socket	For TR2 (Digi-Key [Keystone] 4601K-ND); include insulating washer
Heat sink	For TR2, 50 watts: Digi-Key HS117; Mouser 334S262. The Mouser heat sink may not be drilled; use the insulating washer as drilling guide
Indicator lamp	Radio Shack 272-337 (optional)
Miscellaneous	Control knob Letraset or similar: Jameco (Datak) 9601, 9621 (for lettering decals) Two-tag terminal strip for resistor Four-position terminals for rectifier-distribution unit: Radio Shack 274-622 or 274-658

needed if you use only one controller. The power-on indicator lamp is optional, but adds to the appearance of the control head.

TR1 is a Darlington transistor (two

transistors in one case), so the circuit has in effect three transistors connected in cascade, giving smoother control and less power loss than the two transistors of the original circuit.

I attached the heat sink, cable, and terminal strip to the case of the control head with ACC. This is something no manufacturer would do, but everything has survived several drops to the

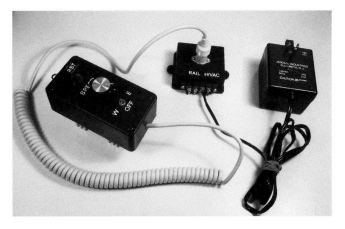

Fig. 4-11. The 2ST—a second-generation simplest transistor throttle in tethered walkaround format.

Fig. 4-12. Interior wiring of the 2ST throttle.

floor. An eyelet at the top of the control head lets it be hung from hooks on the benchwork.

Wiring

The rectifier-distribution unit contains only the bridge rectifier, the overload protection device, four screw terminals, and a DIN 5-pin plug for connection. Connect two screw terminals to the AC connections of the bridge rectifier, one via the overload protection device F. Connect the other two screw terminals to two DIN pins, which will be connected through the cable to the direction switch in the control head. You may need a meter to check which pins they are, because the color code of the cable may not be obvious at both ends. Connect the positive and negative leads of the bridge rectifier to the DIN pins that go to positive and negative in the control head. Check the cable at each end with a meter to ensure no crossed wires.

❑ Cut a diamond-shaped hole in the cover plate of the control head so the socket and heat sink for TR2 can be mounted on the outside. See fig. 4-12 for the overall view and fig. 4-7 for details of mounting.

❑ Solder the C lead of TR1 directly to the C lead of TR2.

❑ Solder the E lead of TR1 directly to the B lead of TR2.

❑ Connect the third lead (B) of TR1 to resistor R.

❑ Connect the other end of resistor R to a flexible wire that goes to the center connection of VR, the speed control.

❑ Connect the C leads of TR1 and TR2 to the right terminal of VR.

❑ Also connect to the right terminal of VR the positive wire of the cable.

❑ Connect the E lead of TR2 to one of the center terminals of S, the direction switch.

❑ Connect the other center terminal of S to the left terminal of VR.

❑ Also connect to the left terminal of VR the negative wire of the cable.

❑ Connect the other two wires of the cable to the cross-connected outer terminals of switch S.

❑ Connect the optional indicator lamp to the outer terminals of VR.

Troubleshooting and testing

The test procedure is the same as for the power pack conversion above.

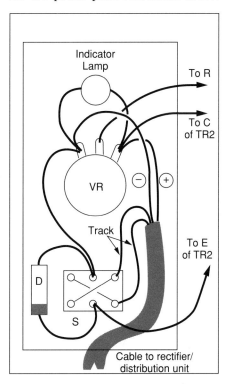

Fig. 4-13. Wiring of the control head for the 2ST.

Take care that the connections at each end of the cable are correct. The output wave form is a smooth pulsating DC at 120Hz (the 1ST was 60Hz). There is no significant motor heating with this wave form, but if you prefer filtered DC, see the next project in this chapter.

Both the previous throttles are 12-volt, and Z scale locomotives are 9-volt. What changes are necessary for Z scale?

Any transistor throttle with a potentiometer speed control can be modified to a lower maximum voltage

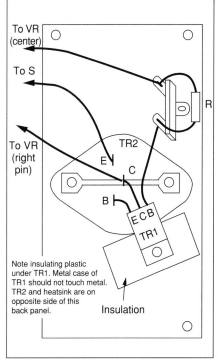

Fig. 4-14. Wiring of the back panel of the control head (left) and the rectifier-distribution unit (right).

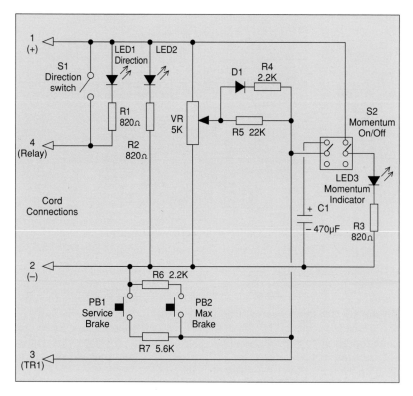

Fig. 4-15. Circuit of the FPW control head. Some values can differ—see the parts list.

PARTS LIST FOR FPW CONTROL HEAD	
Plastic enclosure	Approximately 5" × 2½" × 1⅝": Radio Shack 276-233; Digi-Key SR033-ND; Hammond 1591LSBK
LED1, 2, 3	Light-emitting diodes—color and size are your choice.
LED mounting clips	3 needed: 3mm, Mouser 352-001; 5mm, 352-002
VR	5,000-ohm, 0.5-watt linear-taper rotary potentiometer: Mouser 31VA305; Radio Shack 271-1714; Jameco 29196
PB1, PB2	Normally open pushbuttons: Radio Shack 275-8077 or 275-1547; Mouser 10PA010, 10PA111
S1	SPST rocker switch: Radio Shack 275-8031; Mouser 10RM001
S2	Miniature DPDT switch, must not be center-off type: Radio Shack 275-633; Mouser 10TC260
D1	Diode, 1N4148: Digi-Key 1N4148PH; Jameco 36038
R1, R2, R3	820-ohm, 0.5-watt resistors
R4	2.2k, 0.5-watt resistor. This resistor in conjunction with D1 produces faster acceleration than deceleration in the momentum position. R4 and D1 can be omitted if you prefer slower acceleration.
R5	22K, 0.5-watt resistor—a higher value gives longer momentum
R6	2.2K, 0.5 watt resistor—a higher value gives longer emergency braking time
R7	5.6K, 0.5-watt resistor—a higher value gives longer service braking time
C1	470µF, 25-volt electrolytic capacitor—a lower value gives shorter momentum times; higher value, longer: Digi-Key (Panasonic) P6350; Mouser (Xicon) 140-XA25V470
Terminal strip	3-position: Mouser 158-004
DIN cable	5-pin type, with plug at one or both ends: Mouser 172-5910 A computer keyboard cable is suitable, as in fig. 4-4: Jameco 22234. You may also use 4-wire modular telephone cable: Digi-Key H1442-25-ND (25 feet, straight); H1442-14C-ND (14 feet, coiled)
Miscellaneous	Control knob, wire

by wiring a fixed resistor in series with the speed control terminal that corresponds to maximum speed (normally the one at the top right as you look at the rear). The value of the resistor should be about 33 percent of the value of the speed control. Thus, for a 5K control, the resistor should be 1.8K (1,800 ohms). For a 2K control, the resistor should be 680 ohms. It's possible instead to reduce the AC input voltage to the throttle, but the resistor method is easier to add to a commercial throttle.

Why can't a fuse be used for overload protection?

A model railroad is a peculiarly nasty environment for throttles because of the innumerable brief accidental (I trust) short circuits. For example a short-wheelbase locomotive traversing a double-slip switch almost invariably creates a couple of track shorts. A metal wheel can bridge a rail gap, and if there's a voltage differential across the gap, the throttle can get the shock of its life.

Such brief shorts would blow a fuse three times a day—and a "slow-blow" fuse would blow twice. Commercial throttles use time-delay devices. Heat in a bimetallic strip enclosed in a glass envelope opens a set of contacts and breaks the circuit. With power disconnected, the strip cools and the device resets itself. This overload protection takes from seconds to minutes to operate, depending on the magnitude of the short circuit current. These glass devices are made by Philips ECG. Part numbers are given in the parts list for the 2ST.

The positive temperature coefficient resistor is another type of overload protection device. It is a thin disk, less than an inch in diameter. Heat caused by excess current passing through it causes its resistance to increase sharply, so the current available is decreased to a safe level. Part numbers for these are also found in the 2ST parts list. With these devices the short must be eliminated before the device resets itself.

Because these protectors take time to operate, the transistors in a solid state throttle are subject to heavy loads for a period. This is why the designs in this book use the transistors, diodes, and SCRs conservatively—probably more conservatively than most commercial designs.

There is another protection device, the three-terminal regulator. It shuts down if overheated or overloaded, but operates only on filtered DC.

I need a long walkaround cable for my garden railroad. Does voltage loss in the cable cause problems?

Yes. A 20-foot telephone extension cord typically has a resistance of 6 or 7 ohms (total for the four wires). A 1-

amp motor will lose 6 or 7 volts in the cable. Therefore the motor current must be kept out of the cable. The throttle below carries only a few milliamps in the cable. Reversing is done by a relay in the base unit, and only the base current of a transistor and indicator LED currents flow in the four-wire cable that connects the control head to the base power unit. You can use a telephone extension cable and connectors without motor voltage loss. The base power unit should not be exposed to weather.

The FPW—Full-performance Walkaround Throttle

This is a filtered DC cab with a small 60-Hertz pulse. With different transformers and resistors it can furnish up to 3 amps at 19 volts. The con-

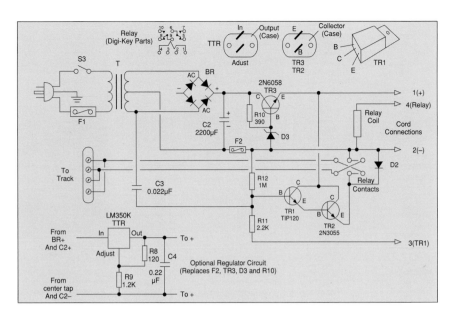

Fig. 4-16. Circuit of the FPW throttle base unit.

PARTS LIST FOR FPW BASE UNIT (FIG. 4-16)			
T	Transformer. 36-volt (CT), 1.5-amp: Digi-Key (Microtran) MT3192-ND 36-volt (CT), 2-amp: Hammond 167L36 36-volt (CT), 3-amp: Hammond 167M36 (this transformer is 3.8" high) 42-volt (CT), 2-amp (for G locomotives): Hammond 165L42.	R10**	390-ohm, 0.5 watt resistor
		R11	2.2K, 0.5-watt resistor
		R12	1M, 0.5-watt resistor
		Relay	DPDT (2 Form C), 5 amps, 12 volts: Digi-Key (P&B) PB125-ND; Mouser 433-2411 For G scale, use a 24-volt relay: Digi-Key (P&B) PB126-ND. The connections shown on the circuit diagram apply only to the Digi-Key relay.
S3	SPST UL-CSA-listed switch: Mouser (Mountain Switch) 10TE005; Radio Shack 275-8010		
F1	2-amp UL-CSA-listed fuse or circuit breaker: Digi-Key F119-ND; fuse holder, F001-ND	Power	3-wire, UL-CSA listed: Mouser 173-33121; cord: Jameco 37997
F2**	3- or 4-amp circuit breaker: Philips ECG204	Terminal strips	1 each 2-lug, 5-lug, and 7-lug: Mouser 158-1002, 158-1005, 158-1007
BR	10-amp, 100-volt bridge rectifier: Mouser 333-MB151; Digi-Key (G.I.) GBPC1001	Metal	Approximately 8" × 6" × 3": Radio Shack 270-274 (painted enclosure steel); Digi-Key (Heeger) L148-ND (aluminum); Mouser (Heeger) 537-146-P (painted aluminum); Jameco 11949 (painted aluminum panel, steel case). The Jameco enclosure is only 2.75" high
C2	2,200µF or 3,300µF, 35-volt electrolytic capacitor: Mouser (Xicon) 140-XA35V2200 or 140-XA35V3300; Digi-Key (Panasonic) P5459 or P5460		
C3	0.022µF, 100-volt film capacitor: Digi-Key (Panasonic) P1004; Mouser (Xicon) 23ME322. This capacitor injects a small pulse into the throttle to improve slow running. An increase to 0.047µF will double the pulse to about 2 volts but may cause creep with some efficient motors.	Heatsinks	For TR3 or TTR—22-watt drilled for TO-3 (TO-44) case: Mouser (Aavid) HS103-.75 For TR2, 100-watt, drilled for TO-3 (TO-44) case: Mouser (Aavid) HS118
		Terminal strip	For track connection: Radio Shack 274-622
		Cord socket	For modular phone cord: Digi-Key (Hirose) H9062 panel mount jack For 5-pin DIN keyboard cable: Digi-Key (Cui Stack) CP-1250-ND; Radio Shack 274-005; Jameco 15843
C4**	0.22µF, 100-volt film capacitor: Digi-Key (Panasonic) P1028; Mouser (Xicon) 23ME422		
TR1	TIP120 NPN Darlington transistor: Mouser 511-TIP120; Digi-Key TIP120GE-ND; Jameco 32993.		
TR2	2N3055 NPN power transistor: Mouser 511-2N3055; Jameco 38308; Radio Shack 276-2041	Miscellaneous	Hardware Color-coded connecting wire Grommet Cable clamp 2 transistor sockets: Digi-Key (Keystone 4601K-ND), 2 washers: Digi-Key (Keystone 4662K-N)
TR3**	2N6058 NPN Darlington transistor: Mouser 511-2N6058		
D2	1N5402 diode: Digi-Key 1N5402; Mouser 333-PG5402; Jameco 77083		
D3**	16-volt, 1-watt Zener diode: Mouser or Digi-Key 1N4745A For G scale, use a 20-volt, 1-watt Zener diode: Mouser or Digi-Key 1N4747A. Remember that Zener diodes are connected backwards, cathode to positive.	** Components F2, TR3, D3, and R10 are not used when the LM350K TTR is used to replace 2N6058 TR3. Components R8, R9, and C4 are added. These are mounted on Tag 1 in positions vacated by F2, D3, and R10. For the circuit, see the side diagram in fig. 4-5A. The LM350K uses the same heat sink as specified for TR3, but the connections are different. When the LM350K TTR circuit variation is used with G scale, resistor R9 must be 1.8K in order to obtain the higher output voltage (18-19 volts).	
TTR**	3-amp 3-terminal positive adjustable regulator, LM350K: Jameco 23931		
R8**	120-ohm, 0.5-watt resistor		
R9**	1.2K, 0.5-watt resistor		

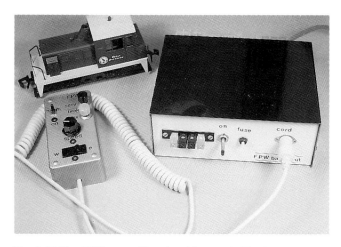

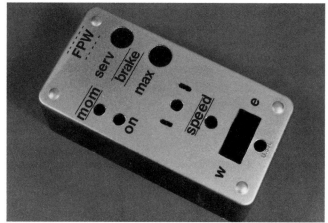

Fig. 4-17. The FPW control head and base unit. The locomotive is O scale.

Fig. 4-18. FPW control head with mounting holes for the controls.

trol head has a momentum switch, pushbuttons for service and maximum braking, and LEDs that indicate power connected, direction, and momentum. The circuit has little transformer loss, and the rectifier DC output is stabilized. Overload protection is through use of a 3-amp TTR; an alternate circuit uses an ordinary power transistor and separate short circuit protection.

Motor current does not flow in the remote control cable, which can therefore be quite long. The unit does not have memory, so the cable must be connected at all times.

Figs. 4-15 and 4-16 show the circuits of the control head and the base unit, which are connected by a four-

Fig. 4-19. Interior of the FPW control head.

wire cable. The base unit has connections to the track and an AC power cord. (In wiring the transformer, be sure to follow all precautions discussed in Chapter 1.) This throttle is not an easy project. There is no printed circuit board because most components are wired between switches or other fixed contacts. I suggest wiring the control head first; it's the easier of the two pieces.

Wiring the control head

Use a plastic box, because there is little or no heat inside and it's easier to file and drill than metal. The drilled panel is shown on fig. 4-18. The VR speed-control holes are for a slot-mounted component; if yours is a nut-mounted item, make a ⅜" hole. The brake pushbuttons specified require ½" holes; the DPDT momentum switch, ¼". I used an SPST rocker switch for direction and filed out a rectangular mounting hole. I used 5mm LEDs mounted in holders that required ¼" holes. The current ratings of the brake pushbuttons and direction and momentum switches are unimportant; these components carry very low currents. Size, shape, and color of the direction and momentum switches, brake pushbuttons, and LEDs are not crucial—you can choose whatever suits you.

The wiring is shown in fig. 4-20. Connect the 820-ohm (gray red brown) LED resistors first. The cathode connection of the LEDs is normally indicated by a flat area on the plastic case.

❑ Connect R1 between the cathode of LED1 and one terminal of S1.

❑ Connect R2 between the cathode of LED2 and the left (negative) terminal of VR.

❑ Connect R3 between the cathode of LED3 and the left terminal of VR.

❑ Connect the anode of LED1 to the right terminal (positive) of VR.

❑ Connect the anode of LED2 to the right terminal (positive) of VR.

❑ Connect the anode of LED3 to one center terminal of S2, the momentum switch.

❑ Connect R6 (2.2K, red red red) between one terminal each of PB1 and PB2, the brake pushbuttons.

❑ Connect R7 (5.6K, green blue red) between the other terminals of PB1 and PB2.

❑ Connect the minus side of C1 to the junction of R6 and PB1.

❑ Connect a wire from this same point to the left (negative) terminal of VR.

❑ Connect a wire from the junction of R7 and PB2 to the other center terminal of S2.

❑ Connect R5 (22K, red red orange) between the two ends of the terminal strip.

❑ Connect R4 (2.2K, red red red) between one end and the middle of the terminal strip.

❑ Connect D1 between the other end and the middle of the terminal strip, with the cathode (the end with a band of color or all the color bands grouped closely) to the middle.

❑ Run a 3" length of wire from the junction of R7 and PB2 to the terminal strip at the junction of R4 and R5.

❑ Connect the positive end of C1 to S2 as shown—the end terminal on the side of the switch that R4 and R5 are connected to.

❑ Connect the other terminal at the same end of S2 to the right terminal of VR.

❑ Connect the center terminal of

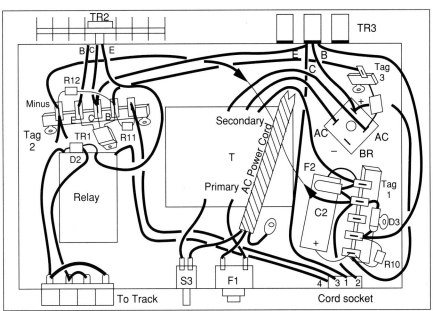

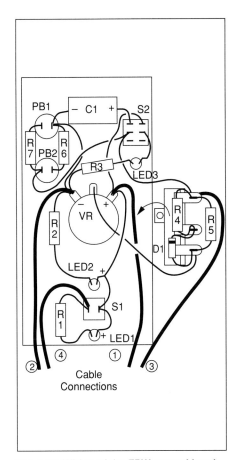

Fig. 4-20. Wiring of the FPW control head.

Fig. 4-21. Wiring of the FPW base unit.

Fig. 4-22. Interior of the FPW base unit.

VR with a 3" wire to the end of the terminal strip at the junction of R5 and D1.

❏ Secure the terminal strip to the case with cyanoacrylate adhesive or epoxy (a nut and bolt would spoil the appearance of the panel).

Now add the four leads of the cable. I used a PC keyboard cable; you can use a four-wire modular telephone extension cable instead. I suggest a coiled cord. Don't use a cable that has extra-fine wire or feels stiff. These are difficult to solder and failure-prone, and I have the pieces to prove it! Watch the color code to ensure the connections at the base power unit come out correctly.

Secure the cable where it enters the control head with a filler cyanoacrylate adhesive adhesive such as Zap-a-Gap. A rubber grommet over the cable and against the inside of the case gives extra adhesive surface.

Base power unit for the FPW

The FPW throttle can produce up to 3 amps, depending on the power transformer. Maximum output voltage is either 12 or 19. There are two options for stabilizing voltage and pro-

tecting against short circuits. The best option is to use the 3-amp TTR, but few distributors stock the LM350K device (Jameco is one). There's also a 5-amp TTR that has identical connections, the LM338K (Jameco part 23835). The transistor regulator (2N6058) is more widely available. The differences are indicated on the parts list. The control head and cable are the same for all versions.

Use figs. 4-19 and 4-21 as wiring guides. The case shown in fig. 4-19 is a steel box from Radio Shack. The front

panel holds the on-off switch, the overload trip, the socket for the interconnect cord, and the track connector panel. The switch requires a ½" hole. If you substitute a fuse for the overload trip, you will need a ⅝" hole instead of ⅜". You can substitute a modular telephone socket for the DIN 5-pin socket that is shown.

TR2 and TR3 are mounted on the rear panel with their sockets, insulating washers, and heat sinks as shown in fig. 4-7. TR2 gets the larger heat sink. Check with a meter to ensure

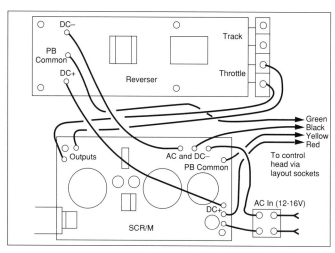

Fig. 4-23. The SCR/M (memory SCR throttle) and the associated remote reverser unit.

Fig. 4-24. Connecting the SCR/M throttle and the reverser. The four color-coded leads go to modular telephone sockets around layout.

that the cases of TR2 and TR3 are insulated from the metal box. You may have to enlarge the mounting holes in the heat sinks so the insulating bushings fit properly. The power cord enters through the rear panel. A ½" hole should be sufficient.

Next install the transformer. Make sure that the transformer you buy fits in the box. The 3-amp Hammond transformer in the parts list is nearly 4" high; the others are less than 3".

The transformers in the parts list are all center-tapped. You may use 18- or 21-volt non-center-tapped transformers (for G scale) and wire the bridge rectifier as a full bridge instead of leaving the negative terminal of the bridge rectifier unconnected. Figure 3-14 in Chapter 3 shows how.

Secure the bridge rectifier and the three terminal strips with screws and nuts. I used silicone sealant to mount the direction relay. I could have made a metal bracket to hold a relay socket, but I thought that would be overkill.

Take care when bending the leads of TR1, D2, and D3. Don't bend leads right at the semiconductor body, but hold the leads at the body with pliers and bend at the other side to avoid stress on the semiconductor body, which could later cause failure

Wiring

❏ Connect one transformer primary lead to one contact of S3 (the on-off switch).

❏ Connect the other primary lead to one lead of F1 (the main fuse).

❏ Connect the center tap of the secondary to the top tag of terminal strip Tag 1.

❏ Connect to that same tag one lead of F2, the low-voltage circuit breaker.

❏ Also connect to that same tag the negative lead of C2.

❏ Connect the other two secondary leads of the transformer to each of the AC pins of BR, the bridge rectifier.

❏ Connect the positive pin of BR with red wires to the lower tag of terminal strip Tag 1. (The color of the wire you use isn't crucial; the colors specified here match the photo.)

❏ Also connect the positive pin of BR to the C lead of TR3.

❏ With red wire connect the E lead of TR3 to terminal 1 (+) of the cable socket.

❏ Again using red wire, connect the E lead of TR3 to the center tag of terminal strip Tag 2.

❏ Run a wire from the center tag of Tag 2 to the C connection of TR2.

❏ Connect the positive lead of C2 to the bottom tag of Tag 1.

❏ Connect the two ends of R10 (orange white brown) between the bottom and next-to-bottom tags of Tag 1.

❏ Also connect to the next-to-bottom tag of Tag 1 the cathode (striped) end of Zener diode D3.

❏ From that same tag run a gray wire to the B connection of TR3.

❏ Connect the anode of D3 to the next-to-top tag of Tag 1.

❏ To that same next-to-top tag of Tag 1 connect the other lead of F2.

❏ From that same tag run a black wire to terminal 2 (-) of the cable socket.

❏ From that same tag run another black wire to the left tag of Tag 2.

❏ From the left tag of Tag 2 run a

black wire to relay pin 1. (In fig. 4-21 these wires stop short of the relay to avoid confusion in a congested area in the diagram.)

❏ Also from the left tag of Tag 2 run a black wire to relay pin 6.

❏ Connect diode D2 between relay pins 6 and 9, with the cathode to pin 9.

❏ From pin 9 of the relay run a brown wire to the E connection of TR2.

❏ Use a green wire to connect relay pins 7 and 8 to one of the track terminals.

❏ Similarly connect relay pins 5 and 10 to the other track terminal.

❏ With a yellow wire connect relay pin 4 to terminal 4 (relay) of the cable socket.

❏ Connect the E, C, and B leads of TR1 to the second, third, and fourth tags of Tag 2.

❏ From the second tag of Tag 2 (the E lead of TR1) run a white wire to the B connection of TR2.

❏ Connect R12 (brown black green) between the first and fourth tags of Tag 2.

❏ Connect R11 (red red red) between the fourth and fifth tags of Tag 2.

❏ Run a white wire from the fourth tag of Tag 2 (the B lead of TR1) to terminal strip Tag 3.

❏ Connect capacitor C3 between Tag 3 and either AC connection of bridge rectifier BR.

❏ Run a gray wire from the right (fifth) tag of Tag 2 to terminal 3 of the cable socket.

❏ The other end of R12 goes to the left tag of Tag 2, where three black wires already await it.

The middle tag of Tag 1 and the

negative lead of the bridge rectifier remain unconnected.

❏ Connect the live lead of the power cord (usually the white one in a power cord) to the remaining terminal of S3.

❏ Connect the neutral lead of the power cord (black) to the remaining terminal of F1.

❏ Anchor the ground lead of the power cord to the metal case using a solder lug under a nut and screw. Use a meter to ensure that no leads are crossed and that the metal case is connected to the ground pin on the plug of the power cord.

❏ Use a grommet and a cable clamp, size depending on the power cord, to anchor the power cord to the back of the box. Don't simply tie a knot in the cord inside the box—it's not a good practice.

Troubleshooting the FPW

The base unit delivers a fixed 12 to 13 volts (18 to 19 volts for the G version) to the control head through two of the four wires in the interconnecting cord. Plug the control head in and set the speed control at maximum. If voltage is not present between pins 1 (positive) and 2 (negative), briefly disconnect the control head. If voltage appears then, it's likely that wires in the interconnect cable are crossed. If voltage is still not present, check for positive voltage at the C lead of TR3 (or IN of the TTR)—about 20 volts (25 for the G version). Check the transformer connections, the line cord on-off switch, and the fuse.

Voltage at the E lead of TR3 (or OUT of the TTR) should be 14 to 15 (20 to 21 for the G version). If not, check wiring of TR3 or TTR.

Voltage at all pins of TR1 and TR2 should be within 12 to 13 (or 18 to 19). If not, check the wiring of TR1 and TR2. If there is still no voltage to the control head, ensure that the connections to D2 are not reversed.

If the other tests are OK, but there is no voltage to the track, check the relay switch connections, especially if you are using a relay other than the one specified. Relay connections can vary considerably between manufacturers.

Now swing the speed control down and up. Voltages at all connections of TR1 and TR2 should follow. If not, check the wiring to VR and see that lead 3 of the cable is not crossed. If the

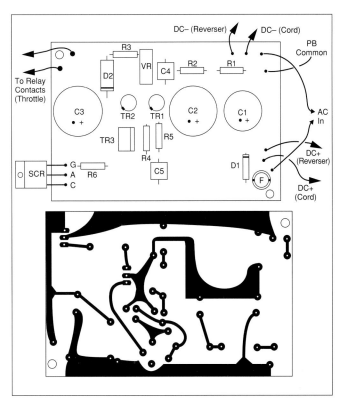

Fig. 4-25. Full-size PC board layout for SCR/M throttle section and component locations.

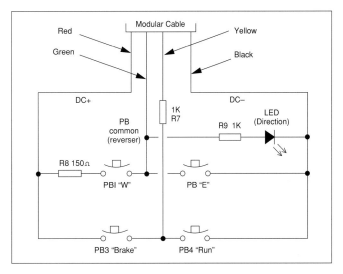

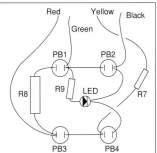

Fig. 4-26. Circuit and wiring diagram for the control head of the SCR/M.

43

momentum switch doesn't work, check that C1 is wired in correct polarity.

Check the brake functions with momentum on. Normal service application fights the throttle; if you increase the throttle you can start to override the brake. If either brake doesn't function, check the pushbuttons (and certainly ensure that they are normally open types, not normally closed).

Check the LEDs. The direction indicator is on when the direction switch is in only one position. The power-on LED should be lit whenever the cable is connected to the base unit. The momentum LED lights only when the momentum is switched on. If an LED doesn't function, check its polarity.

What does the pulse switch on a throttle do?

A few years back, when DC motors were miniature versions of horse-power-rated real-life motors, there was a considerable advantage to adding a vibration pulse on top of the nominally DC throttle voltage. This overcame "stiction"—sticky bearings, binding siderods on steam locomotives, and cogging. Cogging occurs as an armature pole (the rotating part) moves in and out of the magnetic field. You can feel cogging if you turn the

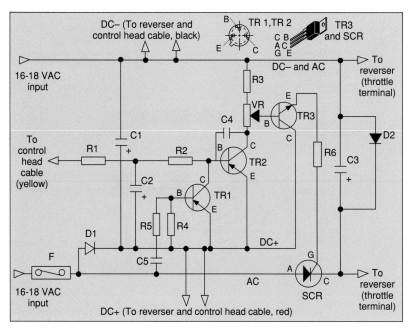

Fig. 4-27. Circuit for the SCR/M throttle unit showing reverser and control head connections.

PARTS LIST FOR SCR/M THROTTLE (FIG. 4-27)	
TR1, TR2	PNP small signal transistor, 2N2907A: Mouser 511-2N2907A; Digi-Key 2N2907A
TR3	NPN medium power transistor: Mouser 511-TIP29; Digi-Key TIP29GE-ND
SCR	12-amp, 200-volt silicon controlled rectifier, 2N6395: Mouser (Teccor) 519-S4012R; Digi-Key (Teccor) S4012R
D1	Rectifier diode, 1N4002: Mouser 333-1N4002; Digi-Key 1N4002GI
D2	Rectifier diode, 1N5402: Mouser 333-1N5402; Digi-Key 1N5402GI
C1	2,200µF, 25- or 35-volt electrolytic capacitor: Mouser (Xicon) 140-XR35V2200; Digi-Key (Panasonic) P6244
C2, C3	4,700µF, 25- or 35-volt electrolytic capacitors: Mouser (Xicon) 140-XR35V4700; Digi-Key (Panasonic) P6246
C4	0.022µF, 100-volt film capacitor: Mouser (Xicon) 140-PF2A223G; Digi-Key (Panasonic) EF1223
C5	0.1µF, 100-volt film capacitor: Mouser (Xicon) 140-PF2A104G; Digi-Key (Panasonic) EF1104
VR	2K or 2.5K trimmer potentiometer: Digi-Key (CTS) X201R252B-ND; Mouser 32RV302 (adjust PCB holes closer with Mouser product)
F	Overload protection, hold at 3 to 4 amps: Philips ECG ECG204 or MB-317; Raychem Polyswitch RBE270A; Digi-Key (Potter & Brumfield) PB184-ND (manual reset, not automatic)
R1	470-ohm, 0.25- or 0.5-watt resistor (yellow purple brown)
R2	470K, 0.25- or 0.5-watt resistor (yellow purple yellow)
R3	2.2K, 0.25- or 0.5-watt resistor (red red red)
R4	5.6K, 0.25- or 0.5-watt resistor (green blue red)
R5	56K, 0.25- or 0.5-watt resistor (green blue orange)
R6	56-ohm, 0.5-watt resistor (green blue black)
	Control Head Components
Enclosure	See text or use Radio Shack 270-230 (3¼" x 2⅛" x 1¹⁄₁₆") or Digi-Key (Heeger) L111-ND
R7, R9	1K, 0.5 watt resistors (brown black red)
R8	150-ohm, 1-watt resistor (brown green brown)
PB1, 2, 3, 4	Normally open single-pole pushbutton switches: Mouser (Mountain Switch) 10PA012, 10PA210 or (thin keyboard type) 10KB010; Digi-Key (Panasonic) P8031S (Keyboard type); Radio Shack 275-1547 or 275-1566; Jameco 26622 (MS102) The thin keyboard types are for use in shallow control head boxes and will need a PCB board for mounting. The other buttons specified are preferable for larger boxes.
LED	Light-emitting diode—any type or color
AC power supply	Radio Shack 273-1511 (12.6 volts, 3 amps, center tap not used) You can use instead a plug-in transformer or a spare Lionel or American Flyer AC power pack set to 13 or 18 volts, depending on whether the required output voltage is 12 or 17 (do not use a solid-state Lionel pack). The SCR / M is good for up to 3 amps. The AC supply determines the voltage ratings of the two relays in the reverser. For up to 14 volts AC input use 12-volt relays; for higher inputs use 24-volt relays.
Relay reverser	See Chapter 3 for PCB layout and parts list.
Miscellaneous	Mounting plate for SCR/M and reverser (metal panel preferred), PCB for SCR/M, Wire, 2-position terminal block: Radio Shack 279-350. Heat sink for SCR: Digi-Key (Aavid) HS115; Mouser (IERC) 567-7-199-BA; Jameco 72346 (MK-541) Dual wall plate with modular telephone sockets: Radio Shack 279-350; Jameco 72311 12' modular phone cord: Radio Shack 279-312; Jameco 72071; Digi-Key H1442-07C-ND

Fig. 4-28. SCR/M control head as modified from a hand-held computer game (the original is at the right).

Fig. 4-29. The control head can also be in a more conventional metal or plastic case. This view shows the wiring.

shaft of a three-pole motor by hand. Most newer DC motors have five or seven poles, and the cogging is much less noticeable. In addition, some motors have skewed armatures so that different parts of the armature move in and out of the field at different times.

Many rheostat throttles had a pulse switch that disconnected one of the two rectifiers, making the output voltage pulse 60 times a second with equal spaces of zero voltage between the pulses. With both rectifiers connected, motor pulses were 120 times a second, with no pauses between them.

The pulse switch improved slow running but reduced the top speed and caused noise and vibration in the motor. Modern DC motors don't require pulse to operate smoothly.

Is it true that SCR throttles are bad and filtered-DC throttles are good?

This question is a continuation of the previous one. The SCR (silicon controlled rectifier) is a controllable diode that can rectify slices of AC to pulsed DC. Most SCR throttles feed a constant 16- to 18-volt pulse to the motor. The width of the pulse varies from very narrow (low energy, low speed) to full width (maximum speed). At maximum speed the output wave form is just like that from the 2ST throttle and is equivalent to 12 volts DC. A narrow pulse, however, creates noise and vibration just like an ordinary throttle with a pulse switch.

Obscured by all the fuss over pulse

is that fact that all you have to do to an SCR throttle is add a large filter capacitor across the output, and the throttle approximates a filtered DC throttle. This is what I've done with one of my older SCR designs, together with adding a full memory feature. This is the next project.

Can a commercial throttle be repaired easily? Mine gives full output all the time.

If it's a transistor throttle, chances are that the transistor has a collector-to-emitter short and must be replaced. Unplug the throttle and open the case. If the case is held together with rivets, drill them out with a ⅛" drill. If you encounter special screwheads beyond the capabilities of your toolbox, use Vise-Grip pliers and replace the screws when you reassemble the throttle.

If the transistor is the same size as a TIP31 or TO-220, replace it with a TIP120 or TIP122, regardless of the number on the case. If it's larger, as in the MRC 6200, use a TIP142, again regardless of the number on the device.

Use thermal grease and maintain any insulation between the aluminum heat sink and the device. Troller throttles (no longer in production and therefore prime candidates for home repair) used a thin brown adhesive film for insulation—it can be reused.

In rare cases the speed control is burnt out because of a base-to-collector short—charring is the clue. Both transistor and speed control (use a 5k

potentiometer as specified for the throttles above) must be replaced if this has happened.

The SCR/M, a memory walkaround throttle

A memory walkaround throttle has a control head that can be unplugged while the operator walks to the next socket and the train continues to run at the same speed in the same direction. The SCR/M (Silicon Controlled Rectifier/Memory) throttle in fig. 4-24 is used with the relay reverser described in Chapter 3. The control

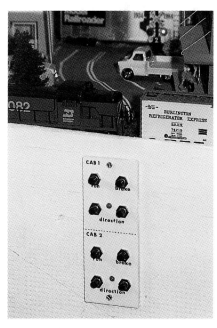

Fig. 4-30. A series of pushbuttons wired in series can be mounted around the layout in lieu of a tethered control head.

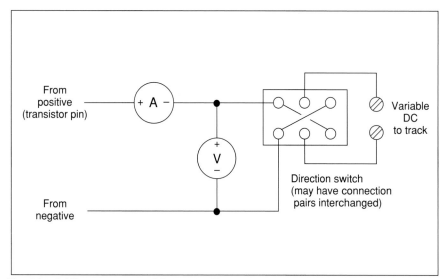

Fig. 4-31. Adding meters to a DC throttle. The ammeter is inserted in the transistor lead formerly going directly to the direction switch. Throttle power indicator lights (if used) remain unchanged.

head contains just three resistors and four pushbuttons, and is connected with a modular telephone cord. An LED in the control head is lit when the control head is plugged in and the train is running in one direction but not the other.

I used the design in *34 New Electronic Projects for Model Railroaders*, but it had a short memory and was a pulse throttle. This version has a 30-minute memory, enough time to go brew a fresh pot of coffee. The pulse is almost completely removed, and the locomotive receives filtered DC.

Pushbutton control has been retained for brake and momentum. Blipping the brake or run pushbuttons allows a slow reduction or buildup of speed; releasing the pushbuttons lets the train continue at the set speed. If either button is held down for two or three seconds, the train quickly reaches full speed or dead stop.

The other two pushbuttons on the control head are the direction control. Pushing either for a second will reverse train direction, one button for east and the other west. The relay reverser unit is described fully in Chapter 3.

The momentum capacitor (C2 in fig. 4-27) has the unusually high value of 4,700μF. The relatively high charge of this capacitor holds the speed when the control head is disconnected; the inherent leakage determines how long it holds the charge. I found that Atlas HO locomotives would run for 30 minutes before slowing to a crawl. The fact that the locomotives eventually stop is an advantage for those who might forget what they were doing before they started making a pot of coffee! A low-leakage capacitor would extend the running period even longer.

Another high-value capacitor (C3, also 4,700μF) is connected across the SCR output and converts its 60Hz output pulses to almost constant DC. The remaining pulse is barely a volt; it would be 20 volts if C3 were absent.

Construction

The SCR/M is assembled on a printed circuit board. Full-size layout and component locations are shown in fig. 4-25; fig. 4-24 shows how the throttle, reverser, and remote control head are connected. The input is 12 to 16 volts AC at 1 to 3 amps (use 16 volts for G scale). I use a 13.7-volt, 2.4-amp wall transformer for my HO locomotives.

If you use a separate power transformer, follow all the safety precautions in Chapter 1. The wiring illustrations for the FPW throttle can also serve as a guide. Do not leave fuse holders exposed. Do not wrap transformer connections in insulating tape and simply fasten the transformer to the underside of the layout. Put all components connected to AC line voltage in a grounded metal box.

Some of the hole positions on the PC board may need to be adjusted—most likely the pin locations for C1, C2, and C3. There is adequate room to move the position of a pin; check after you've obtained the components and before you lay out the PC board.

TR1 and TR2 are PNP transistors. TR3 is an NPN. Note the positions carefully for these. The small tab pro-

Fig. 4-32. The PBU (Prototype Braking Unit) may be connected to most momentum-equipped transistor throttles.

Fig. 4-33. Interior of the PBU.

truding from the case of TR1 and TR2 denotes the emitter pin (the E terminal). The metal side of TR3 faces into the board; the metal side of the SCR faces out. The heat sink for the SCR is small. It doesn't need to be insulated, so the SCR has only a thin film of thermal grease between it and the sink and is bolted on. The heat sink must not touch any other metal part.

Note also the cathode (banded) end of D1 and D2. Ensure that the polarities of C1, C2, and C3 are correct. Diode D1 and capacitor C1 produce filtered DC for the relays in the reverser panel, apart from functioning in the SCR/M.

Two wires run from both the DC positive and DC negative terminals on the SCR/M board. One of each pair goes to the reverser, the other to the remote cable. Another wire from the SCR/M is the common run and brake pushbutton feed. The fourth wire in the remote cable is the common direction pushbutton feed from the reverser to the control head. I color-coded the four wires to the control head to correspond to the color code in the telephone cord—red, positive; black, negative; green, reverser; and yellow, run/brake.

Control head

The control head (figs. 4-26 and 4-28) has only a few components, which allows a lot of personal choice in how it looks and feels. I modified a Radio Shack hand-held computer game. It proved cheaper than a standard plastic case; I junked the circuit board inside but kept the two free batteries that came with it. Fig. 4-29 shows a regular metal case with ordinary pushbuttons (they are viewed from the rear). An alternative is to locate pairs of pushbuttons around the layout.

Testing

When you first power up the throttle, with AC input, reverser, and control head connected, adjust the potentiometer (VR) to maximum resistance. (You can work this out by observing the position of the slider on the carbon track.) VR is an adjustment for maximum speed and will only need to be adjusted if speed is excessive.

Connect a motor or a 12-volt automotive lamp to the track connections, hold down the run button, and the motor should accelerate to full speed or lamp should light to full brightness

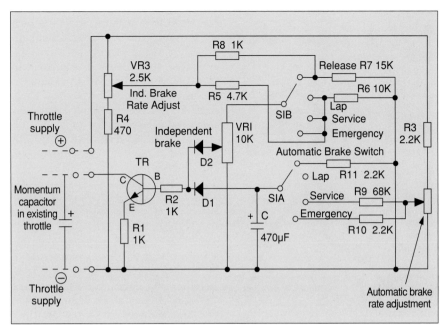

Fig. 4-34. Schematic of the PBU. VR1, S1A, and S1B are the braking controls.

PARTS LIST FOR PBU BRAKE UNIT (FIG. 4-34)

VR1	10K linear potentiometer: Mouser 31VA401; Jameco 29081(P10K); Radio Shack 271-1715)
VR2	10K trimming potentiometer: Digi-Key (CTS 201) U201R103B-ND
VR3	2.5K trimming potentiometer: Digi-Key (CTS 201) U201R252B-ND
	If you use other potentiometers for VR2 and VR3 you will have to revise the PC board layout.
TR	NPN small-signal transistor, 2N2222A: Digi-Key 2N2222A; Mouser 511-2N2222A
D1, D2	Silicon diodes, 1N4148: Digi-Key 1N4148PH; Mouser 592-1N4148; Radio Shack 276-1122
C	470µF, 25-volt electrolytic capacitor: Digi-Key (Panasonic) P5247; Radio Shack 272-1030; Jameco 31181 (R470/25)
S1A/B	2-pole, 6-position rotary wafer switch: Radio Shack 275-1386; Mouser 10YD026; Digi-Key EG1954-ND (connections are different from those illustrated)
Connector	Three-prong: Mouser plug 17HR803 and 16HR633; Digi-Key (Cui Stack) plug CP-1030-ND and socket CP-1230-ND
Enclosure	Approximately 5" × 2½" × 1⅝": Radio Shack 270-233; Mouser (Eagle) 400-1571
R1, R2, R8	1K, 0.5-watt resistors (brown black red)
R3, R10, R11	2.2K, 0.5-watt resistors (red red red)
R4	470-ohm, 0.5-watt resistor (yellow purple brown)
R5	4.7K, 0.5-watt resistor (yellow purple red)
R6	10K, 0.5-watt resistor (brown black orange)
R7	15K, 0.5-watt resistor (brown green orange)
R9	68K, 0.5-watt resistor (blue gray orange)
Miscellaneous	Control knobs (two)
	Hardware
	PCB material (3" × 2¼")

in seconds. Holding down the brake button should stop the motor or extinguish the lamp fast. Check that the relays operate and release when the direction pushbuttons are pressed.

If there are problems, check the DC positive and negative output of the SCR/M. This should read from about 17 volts (with 12 volts AC input) to around 25 volts (with 18 volts AC input). Causes of incorrect voltage

could be lack of AC input, a defective tripped overload protector (F), or D1 or C1 wired backwards. The DC voltage across C2 should go to full DC voltage if the run button is pressed and drop to zero if the brake button is pressed. If not, check the wiring to buttons. The voltages between C and E of TR1, and between B and E of TR2 should also track the DC voltage across C2, though at a slightly lower voltage. If

47

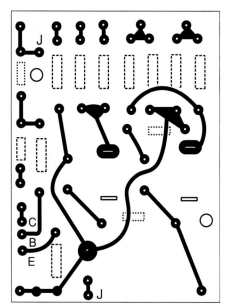

Fig. 4-35. Full-size PC board layout for the PBU.

not, check the orientation of the pins of TR1 and TR2. Plastic-cased substitutes for these transistors may be available, and plastic cases come in two different pin configurations—unless you are sure of what you have, stick with the metal-cased versions specified in the parts list

Both TR3 and the SCR remain quite cool normally. If either overheats and the throttle does not operate, check their connections. If D2 is wired in reverse, it will throw a short circuit across the throttle output—maybe you should check that first!

Are amp and volt meters useful?

Meters are useful to monitor locomotive performance. Starting voltage and stall current can be measured, and bad connections such as dirty brushes can be detected. Short circuits are immediately obvious as the current meter surges to full scale, even

for momentary shorts caused by trackwork. (You may want to fine-tune your track to eliminate them.)

Where do I connect them?

Fig. 4-31 shows the location for the meters. Except for center-zero meters, they are wired ahead of the direction switch on the power-supply side so that they read from left to right, regardless of the direction switch.

Moving-coil meters have a very-low-current movement (such as 1 milliamp for full scale). Resistors are added either in series to make them voltmeters or in parallel to turn them into ammeters. Usually the resistors are inside the meter casing. Meters are often qualified as 1,000 ohms per volt. A 12-volt meter so described has a fixed resistor of just under 12,000 ohms (12K).

Mouser offers 2-inch panel meters appropriate for model railroading. No. 541-MSQ-DVV-015 is a 15-volt DC voltmeter, and 541-MSQ-DAA-005 is a 5-amp DC ammeter.

We have throttles that simulate the prototype—how about brakes?

Prototype brake stands have two levers, one for automatic (train) brakes and the other for independent (locomotive) brakes. Few commercial cabs have anything more than a spring-loaded switch for brake simulation. In the August 1968 issue of *Model Railroader* Dennis Blunt described a half-size model of a KH-6 diesel brake stand built of pine and Masonite. Inside were the electronics to simulate the independent and automatic brakes of the prototype. It could be connected to any transistor momentum throttle with just three leads and required no separate power source. I updated Blunt's circuit and put it in a plastic enclosure for the sake of simplicity. If you want to duplicate the KH-6 brake stand, full plans were in that issue of MR, and a diagram is shown in fig. 4-37.

The circuit of the PBU (Prototype Braking Unit) is in fig. 4-34. The unit connects to a throttle with three leads shown on the left of the circuit. One lead goes to the positive DC in the throttle (usually one side of the speed potentiometer), the second to the positive terminal of the momentum capacitor (usually 220µF, 25-volt), and the third to the negative DC (usually the other side of the speed control or the

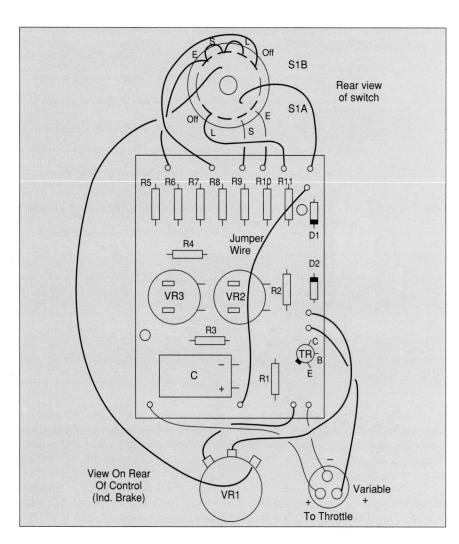

Fig. 4-36. Component location and wiring diagram for the PBU.

Fig. 4-37. The prototype KH-6 brake stand. The independent brake handle is below the automatic on switcher brake stands as it then falls closer to the engineer's hand. The independent, or engine, brake is more important during switching.

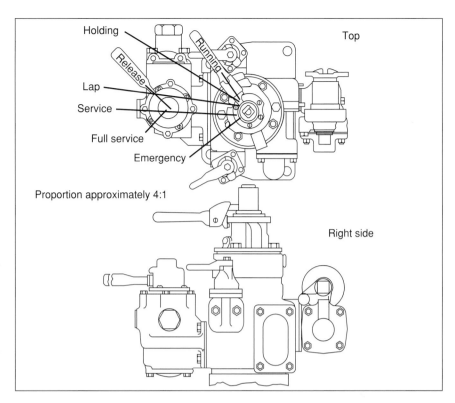

negative terminal of the momentum capacitor. A meter helps, if you're not sure which connections are positive and which negative).

The PBU uses a transistor to bleed the momentum capacitor of the throttle, much as the prototype brake valve bleeds air pressure to slow down. Potentiometer VR1 controls the independent brake. The speed at which the brake works is governed by an adjustable control, VR3. The automatic brake is a two-pole, four-position rotary switch (S1A and S1B). The four positions are labeled Run, Lap, Service, and Emergency. S1B modifies the action of the independent brake in the Service and Emergency positions to slow its action in the case of a simulated long train, when the independent or locomotive brake might be used in addition to the automatic or train brake. Resistors R6, R7, R8, and R9 do this. The automatic brake also has a pre-set adjustment for speed of operation, VR2. Both the adjustment potentiometers slow the respective brake actions when turned clockwise, as viewed from the rear of the PBU.

Capacitor C, in effect a secondary momentum capacitor, produces the delay action of the automatic brake. The momentum switch in the throttle should always be in the on position, but there is no need to use the throttle brake; the independent brake in the PBU provides a braking action equivalent to momentum off in the throttle.

The Run position releases the brakes; the train will not run if either brake is not returned to this position after braking. Although, as in the prototype, the throttle fights the brake, there isn't enough push to overcome locked anchors! The Lap position maintains braking action without change. Moving the knob from Service (normal braking) to Lap maintains the selected speed. Service position gives the effect of braking a heavy train. Emergency (often called Big Hole) stops the train almost immediately.

Wiring the PBU

The enclosure has two ⅜" holes for the brake controls and a ⅝" hole for the interconnect socket. There are also two ⅜" holes in the aluminum back panel to provide access to the VR2 and VR3. Unless you use a larger enclosure than the ones specified in the parts list, the wires connecting the two brake controls must be soldered before the PC board is fitted fully into the enclosure. I used two long screws and spacers to secure the board after wiring. To avoid drilling holes for them in the front of the enclosure, I used epoxy to secure the screw heads against the inside.

The full-size printed circuit board layout is in fig. 4-35. Component locations and wiring for the brake controls and the connection to the throttle are in fig. 4-36. Insert the leads of all the components in the holes on the board. Be careful with the polarities of C, TR, D1, and D2.

❑ Attach six 2" to 3" pieces of insulated copper wire to top of the board.

❑ Connect the other ends to S1A and S1B.

❑ Add jumper wire between the points on the board labeled J.

❑ Use a 5" length of wire to connect S1B to the right terminal of VR.

❑ Use 4" lengths of wire to connect the other terminals of VR to the PC board.

❑ Connect the three wires for the interconnect socket to the throttle.

Color-code them or keep a note of the socket numbers.

After soldering all connections, you can fit the PC board into the enclosure, which should be at least 1½" deep so the underside of the PC board does not touch the brake connections.

Testing

Test the PBU by wiring the three input connections to a dummy throttle—a 47K resistor and a 220µF capacitor connected in series across a 9-volt battery. Connect the positive side of the PBU to the positive terminal of the battery, the negative to the negative, and the third lead to the junction of the resistor and capacitor for this test. Connect a voltmeter across this capacitor to see whether the voltage decreases and increases slowly or rapidly as it tracks the braking action.

Any problems are likely to be from wrong polarity. If you substitute a plastic-cased transistor for the metal-cased one specified, be sure the connections are correct. The same goes if you substitute for switch S1, which is a six-position switch (two-pole, four-position switches are rare). You may want to fabricate a mechanical stop so that you don't overrun the working positions during operation.

5 Switch Machines, Turnouts, and Route Selection

Fig. 5-1. Six typical switch machine motors. Across the top are motorized low-powered slow-motion units. The three below are typical high-powered instant items.

UNLESS YOU ARE just running trains around the Christmas tree once a year, you need to select routes. Yards, industry sidings, passing sidings, and reversing loops all require route selection. You can select the route mechanically (you pull a lever that moves the points) or electrically (you press a button that actuates a solenoid or motor).

The electrically operated versions are popular, especially for operating turnouts that are out of easy reach. Electronic control of the electrically operated part of the turnout is also popular; it makes things much more reliable. As turnout motors (or switch machine solenoids, depending on where you obtained your basic railroad vocabulary) are frequently under the layout, with the wires soldered in position, they are at zero in the popularity contest when model railroaders are at play. Electronics will fix it!

How does electronics improve switch-machine reliability?

Electrically speaking, there are two methods of turnout operation: by DC motors and by AC or DC operated solenoids. A solenoid switch machine consists of a pair of tube-shaped electromagnets with a movable soft iron core or armature. Energize one coil and the iron core slams into the coil. Energize the other coil, and whammo! the core slams to the other end. These solenoids require a large amount of energy for a short time. Unless the power is shut off promptly after they operate, they will burn out. Some have built-in contacts to disconnect the power, but the contacts are somewhat primitive and tend to wear out. Most do not have even this much protection and rely on the operator releasing the pushbutton control switch. Do not locate pushbuttons where a weary elbow might rest! Solenoids can oper-

ate from AC or DC. Most modelers use the auxiliary AC terminals of their power packs as the power source.

Electronics definitely increases the reliability of the solenoids through the use of capacitor discharge power supplies and SCRs (silicon controlled rectifiers). The first eliminates the possibility of burnout of the solenoids and enables small power supplies to throw many turnouts; the second protects the pushbuttons.

When electronics interfaces with solenoids, the operation is DC, and although the auxiliary AC terminals of the power pack can still be used, a rectifier and a filter capacitor are necessary.

What are the pros and cons of solenoids and motor-drive switch machines?

Fig. 5-1 shows three popular motorized types (top) and three solenoid types (below). The differences stem from the difference in power required to operate them. A measure of resistance shows this. From left to right and from top to bottom, the DC-only motorized units are:
PFM/Fulgurex (25-ohm motor)
Mann-Made (20-ohm motor)
Tortoise (Circuitron) (300-ohm motor)

The solenoid types are:
Tenshodo-type (2 ohms)
Peco (4 ohms)
Atlas no. 65 (3.75 ohms)

The motorized units take 2 to 5 seconds to operate. They work on 6 to 12 volts filtered or unfiltered DC, and therefore require a separate power source. Power requirements are specified on the data sheets that come with the machines.

The solenoids snap into operation. The usual twin-coil machine (such as the Tenshodo machine) draws about 8 amps from a 16-volt AC or DC supply for a fraction of a second. Peco and Atlas machines take about half that.

PARTS LIST FOR CD UNITS (FIG. 5-2)

D1, D2*	Rectifier diodes, 1N4004: Mouser 333-1N4004; Digi-Key 1N4004GI; Radio Shack 276-1103 For the heavy-duty unit D2 should be a 1N5404 diode.
D3	Rectifier diode 1N5404: Mouser 333-1N5404; Digi-Key 1N5404GI; Radio Shack 276-1154
TR	NPN power transistor MJE3055T: Mouser 511-MJE3055T; Radio Shack 276-2020) For other than the high-power unit, you may substitute a TIP131 transistor: Mouser 511-TIP131; Digi-Key TIP31PH-ND
R1, R2	470-ohm, 1-watt resistor: Digi-Key (Yageo) 470W-1; Mouser (TransOhm) 29SJ901-470
C1	2,200µF, 25-volt electrolytic capacitor: Digi-Key (Panasonic) P6244; Mouser (Xicon) 140XR25V2200
C2	2,200 or 3,300µF, 25-volt axial-lead electrolytic capacitor: Digi-Key (Panasonic) P6352; Mouser (Xicon) 140-XA25C2200 For the heavy-duty unit C2 should be a 4,700µF, 50-volt capacitor: Digi-Key (Panasonic) P6520; Mouser (Xicon) 140XR50V4700
Miscellaneous	4-terminal terminal strip: Radio Shack 274-622 or (as in photos) 274-679 sliced into 4-terminal parts
Power source	24- to 26-volt, 0.4- to 0.6-amp transformer: (Mouser (HiQ) 41LK600; Jameco (Stancor) 74190 (P-8396); Hammond 166 G25)

The transformer must be enclosed, grounded, fused, and wired as described in Chapter 1. All safety precautions must be taken with the 110-volt connections.

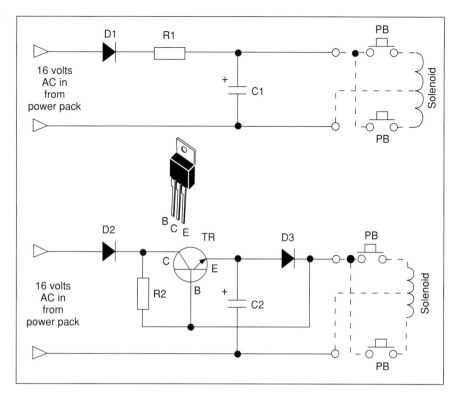

Fig. 5-2. Capacitor discharge switch machine power supplies. The fast-recharge version is below, the 3-second-recharge version above.

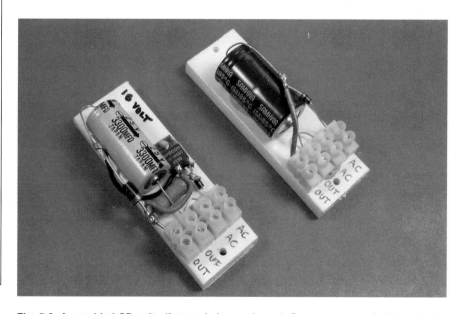

Fig. 5-3. Assembled CD units (fast and slow recharge). Components are held on plastic edge-trim material with silicone cement.

In contrast, the motorized types draw perhaps 0.25 amp from a 6-volt supply. The Tortoise draws 16 milliamps or so and is left in circuit at all times. Its power consumption is so low there is no danger of damage, unlike the solenoid types which can and will self-destruct from overheating if not disconnected after their milliseconds of operational frenzy.

Solenoids require heavy-duty power supplies and heavy-gauge connecting wire because of their high current surge. The motorized units don't.

Solenoids can destroy pushbuttons because of the heavy surge current. Motors don't. Sounds like case proven for motors? Not necessarily—electronics can even up the score.

What is a capacitor discharge (CD) switch machine power supply? What does it do?

A CD power supply consists of a large capacitor, which is charged from a small power supply and then discharges through the pushbutton to the solenoid for operation. If the pushbutton jams or is accidentally held down, or if the solenoid limit switches are stuck, no damage can result because the capacitor cannot recharge.

Fig. 5-2 shows the circuits for two types of CD units. One consists simply of a resistor-capacitor combination; the other adds a transistor, a diode,

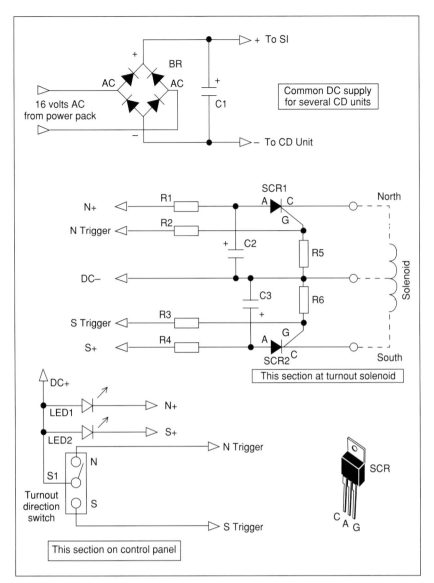

Fig. 5-4. CD System for solenoids needs no heavy wire and has memory direction panel lights.

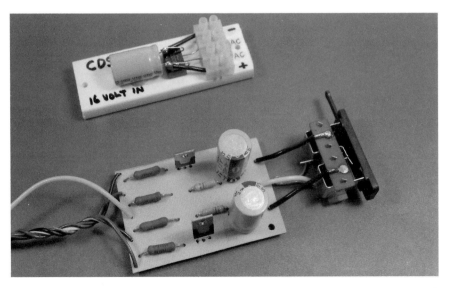

Fig. 5-5. The CD System connected to a Peco PL-12 adaptor base. Also shown is the DC filtered power supply, which will operate up to 20 CD System units.

and another resistor. The latter recharges faster. The difference between the cheap version and the deluxe isn't as great as you may have heard. The simple circuit (with the values shown) will recycle in 3 seconds; the other in less than 1 second. Unless you operate a yard the way some people play the piano, you shouldn't notice the difference.

Is there an advantage to commercial heavy-duty CD units?

These are assemblies with high-value capacitors, operating usually from more than 16 volts. They will operate several solenoid switch machine motors simultaneously and are therefore useful in route control systems where yard routes are selected and groups of machines operate together (see below).

Typical component values for such a unit, based on fig. 5-2, are included in the parts list. The switch machines should all be the same type for simultaneous operation; otherwise the lower-resistance solenoids get the lion's share of the power jolt.

Which type of turnout machine is more reliable?

Dave Sovey of the California Central Model Railroad Club reported in the February 1988 issue of *Model Railroader* that twin-coil solenoids (the usual type) developed mechanical problems between 20,000 and 25,000 cycles. The right-angle links fractured and the center-pivot guide post tended to slip out of its bearing. (Neither the Peco nor the Atlas has these components.)

The motor-drive machines seemed to need jarring every 3,000 to 7,000 cycles. They weren't defective, just needed a tap, possibly because of slight bearing misalignment.

The PFM/Fulgurex machine fared best of all, with no problems in a sample tested to over 100,000 operations. Before making any judgment call, calculate how many years on your layout correspond to 20,000 turnout operations! I bet the pushbuttons won't last as long as the switch machines.

Construction of CD Units

Fig. 5-3 shows the simple unit (right) and the transistor unit (left). Wiring is simple; you can use the photos as a guide. I used a 1¼" × 3¾" piece of plastic edging strip as a component support. It comes in 6-foot lengths at building supply stores. The components, including the terminal strip, can be attached with either silicone cement or a building adhesive such as PL600. The low voltages used give no danger of shock. The units can be simply mounted under the layout or behind the control panel.

How do I wire lights on the control panel to indicate which way a turnout is thrown?

Many switch machines have auxiliary contacts that can be used for indicator lamps. The lamps will have memory—when you power up the layout after a week's vacation, the turnout indicators will be as they were when you switched off the power. Frequently these auxiliary contacts are required for other purposes, such as signaling or switching track power.

The Tortoise machine has a useful feature: a pair of LEDs can be wired in series with one motor lead. Because the motor stalls and remains powered at the end of the operating cycle (but draws only 16 milliamps when it stalls), these LEDs indicate with memory the position of the turnout. The circuit (fig. 5-7) can't be used with other motorized units because they draw too much current for LEDs and cut off the power at the end of the operating cycle.

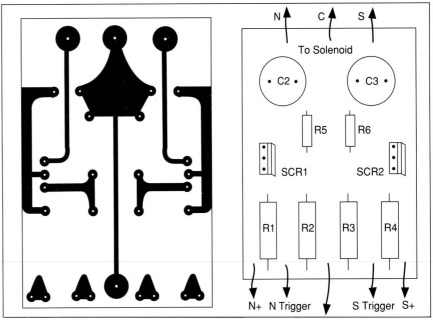

Fig. 5-6. Full-size PC board layout and component locations for CD System.

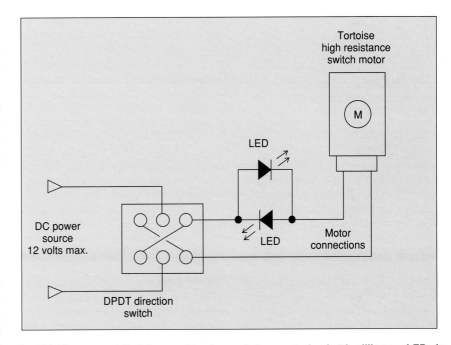

Fig. 5-7. The unusual Tortoise machine has a stall current of only 16 milliamps. LEDs in series with motor can show the position of the switch.

Another simple way is in fig. 5-8. This is a mechanical method using a DPDT slide switch and finger power. Resistor R1 is 1k, 0.5 watt, and the LEDs should be rated at 20 milliamps. You can use the extra contacts on the switch for track power or signals.

The complete CD system

Transistors and integrated circuits have been proposed for controlling panel lamps. Among the circuits published in *Model Railroader* was one that required a separate battery for memory purposes and another, a two-transistor "flip flop," that lacked memory—each time the layout was powered up, all the turnouts had to be operated once to establish correct direction indications. There is a way to combine solenoid switch machines, low pushbutton currents, and LED control panel indicators with memory.

The CD System (fig. 5-4) places a CD unit close to the turnout. The unit has two capacitors, one for each coil of the solenoid. A coil is energized by a positive voltage applied to the gate

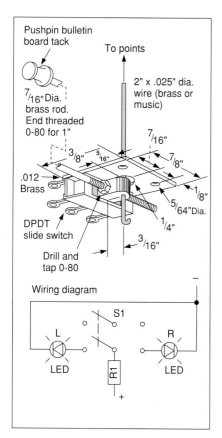

Fig. 5-8. Simple mechanical turnout operation as designed by Fred Miller.

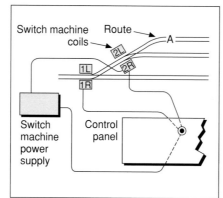

Fig. 5-9. Route A wired with no problem.

contact of an SCR (silicon controlled rectifier). This positive voltage is applied through switch S1 to either SCR1 or SCR2, depending on the position of S1. The SCR is normally held in the off condition by resistor R5 (or R6), which holds the gate trigger at negative. The positive turn-on voltage is applied to the gate trigger through S1 and resistor R1 (or R3).

Switch S1 doesn't have a center-off position, so one SCR is always switched on and the other is off. The LED panel indicator for the SCR that is on lights from the positive supply, through R1 (or R3), the SCR, and the appropriate solenoid coil to negative.

While one SCR is on, the other is always off and its capacitor charges. However as soon as S1 is flipped, the "off" SCR is turned on and the "on" SCR is turned off. (The positive gate trigger has gone to the other SCR.) The SCR that has been switched discharges the capacitor into the solenoid coil, and the turnout flips.

The feature of this circuit is that the SCR turns off because emptying the capacitor causes the anode voltage to collapse temporarily. Once off, the SCR cannot be switched on again until the anode voltage is restored. But this circuit leaves the positive gate trigger on, so the SCR stays on even without significant anode voltage. The LED indicator now lights for this SCR, while the other is extinguished because the other SCR is off.

In addition, the currents carried by the wires to the SCR circuit board are small—20 milliamps maximum. Wires can be long and thin. The control switch itself also carries this low current and is in no danger of damage. In addition to the LEDs, the switch itself indicates turnout direction. Memory is inherent for the lamps and the switch.

When the switch is thrown, the solenoid operates immediately, because the capacitor on the other side of the circuit is charged. The only possible delay might occur if the turnout switch were to be alternated rapidly.

A DC power supply is required; it is shown in fig. 5-4. Connected to the auxiliary 16-volt AC output of a small spare power pack (rated 16 VA or higher), it will supply up to twenty units. If you use but two or three CD Systems, a power pack in use as throttle will have adequate spare current capacity from its AC terminals.

The full-size PC board layout is shown in fig. 5-6 along with the component locations. Be sure to insert the SCRs with their metal sides located correctly, and watch the polarity of C2 and C3. The CD system board should be located right at the turnout.

Problems?

The Peco machine shown has an attached PL-12 adaptor base. The spring in this adapter puts a heavier load on the CD System than a turnout alone. The value of C2 and C3 in the parts list will operate any combination of adapter and turnout, but if you are using most Atlas motors and turnouts, C2 and C3 can be reduced to 1,000μF with a slight cost saving.

Should the CD System fail to trigger, it is likely because of an SCR with an unusually high gate current requirement. Reducing R2 or R3 to 680 ohms will help. I have specified regular SCRs, not the sensitive-gate type.

Can turnouts be operated as a group?

Yes, but a fair dump of power is required, especially with the solenoid

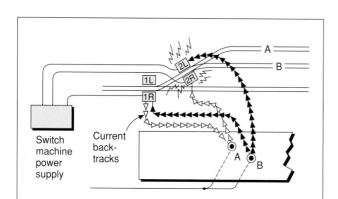

Fig. 5-10. You'll have trouble when you try to wire route B.

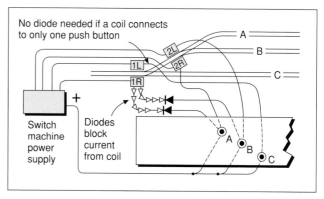

Fig. 5-11. A pair of diodes solves the problem.

switch machines. The heavy-duty CD unit described above is a suitable starting point, as it can operate five or six Peco, Atlas, or other low-power solenoids. The auxiliary contacts on motor-drive machines can be used to operate machines in succession, but with more than three or four machines you run into time limitations.

Position yourself on the yard lead in fig. 5-9, looking in toward the turnouts. Call the directions the points can move L for left and R for right. If the points move to the right, the train goes to the left. Pressing button A is fine. The R coil of each machine is energized and the turnouts direct an incoming train to track A.

Now look at fig. 5-10. Button B sends current to 2L—no problem there—and 1R, but current going to coil 1R from button B can sneak back to coil 2R via button A. Both coils of switch machine 2 are energized. This does the switch machine no good and probably results in the turnout not moving.

If you use DC to power the switch machines, you can use diodes to block the sneak path—see fig. 5-11. Route C presents no problem; coil 1L is connected to only one button and therefore has no sneak paths.

What are the rules for route selection in complex yards?

A more complex yard is shown in fig. 5-12. The six possible routes and the corresponding pushbuttons are labeled A through F, and the turnouts are numbered 1 through 5. The chart shows which coils are energized for each route. Any coil that is used by more than one route constitutes a sneak path and needs a diode between the button and the coil. Column 1R, for example, shows that diodes must be wired downstream from buttons A, B, C, and D.

In the example shown, 10 diodes are needed. The wiring is shown in fig. 5-13. The maximum number of solenoids thrown at the same time is three (routes A, B, and C). This is well within the capacity of a heavy-duty CD unit—and even of the regular CD unit in the lower part of fig. 5-2 if C2 is a 3,300µF component.

The pushbuttons are another matter. They have to pass current for up to three machines at once. Check the switch data in Chapter 3.

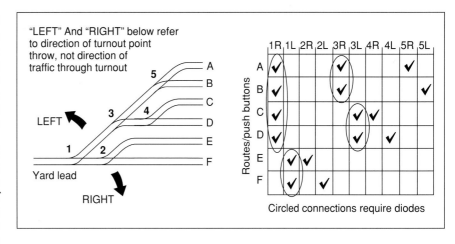

Fig. 5-12. Planning diagram for a diode matrix system.

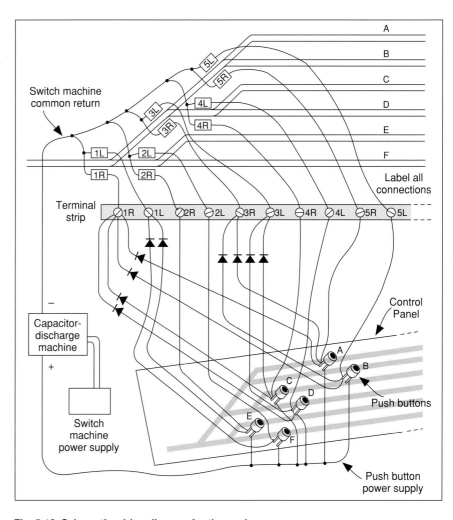

Fig. 5-13. Schematic wiring diagram for the yard.

Wire gauge and distance from turnouts to control panel may also be critical. The common positive connections to the buttons and the common negative return from the machines can also carry a triple load. For any but the smallest layout I recommend 14-gauge wire and good solid double-sided barrier terminal strips such as Mouser (Magnum) 504-TB100-10.

Label those wires! If there are problems, it makes checking easier. Diode polarity is critical, so double-check the cathode stripes.

6 Train Detection

Fig. 6-1. The double Twin-T circuit board.

MODEL TRAINS draw power from the rails. You can control where they run, but sometimes you need the trains to tell you where they are. You may want the trains to operate signals, run backward and forward automatically on a pre-set route, automatically stop at a station, trigger crossing flashers and gates, or slow automatically for sharp curves.

There are three principal ways to detect trains: by the current they draw, by light, and by magnetic field—that is, by electronic circuitry alone or in conjunction with photocells or magnetic reed switches.

The detectors usually activate lights on the control panel, signals on the layout, and relays that switch other circuits. This chapter explains the electronics involved in those devices and explains in detail the Tunnel Tracker and the Twin-T detector, which can tell you where a train is located in a long tunnel or concealed helix.

What's the best train detector circuit?

It depends on system that powers the trains and what modifications you are willing to make to locomotives and cars.

The Twin-T detector will detect anything that will conduct electricity between the rails: locomotives, lighted cars, and cars modified with a 47-kilohm resistor across one set of conducting wheels. The power supply is not detected, so the Twin-T is a true detector of rolling stock in a selected block. The Twin-T has memory. When power is switched off, then restored later, the Twin-T still indicates wherever rolling stock is standing. One drawback is having to install those resistors and conductive wheelsets. Another is that rail gaps are necessary—in both rails, even with a common-rail wiring.

A block-in-use detector is a simpler form of Twin-T that indicates also if the power pack is connected to the block. There are the same drawbacks of having to install resistors and conductive wheelsets and cut rail gaps, and you may not want a device that indicates an empty block is occupied just because the block selector switch is connected to that block.

Three types of detectors that use transistor circuitry are electrically independent of the rails and can be used with command control, high-frequency lighting, and sound-through-the-rails. One type of detector uses magnetic reed switches between the rails, requiring that you secure a small magnet under each locomotive; the second uses photocells and room lighting (sometimes bolstered with a small light nearby); and the third uses infrared transmitters and detectors. The infrared system isn't subject to fluctuations in room light, but at present it is difficult to find the necessary far-infrared light sources and detectors.

The Twin-T doesn't always work the way the books say it should. Why?

The Twin-T track detection circuit was first published in the June, July, and August 1958 issues of *Model Railroader* by Linn H. Westcott. Among the potential problems he documented were the occasional leaky transistor (and the way the circuit works, it is the other transistor that appears to be defective) and minor short circuits that are almost undetectable (a stray spike or bit of screen wire, for example). Other problems have surfaced in the past 35 years. One book on model railroad electronics (not published by Kalmbach) had a Twin-T circuit that couldn't function at all.

Fig. 6-2 shows a basic Twin-T wiring diagram for two blocks and two

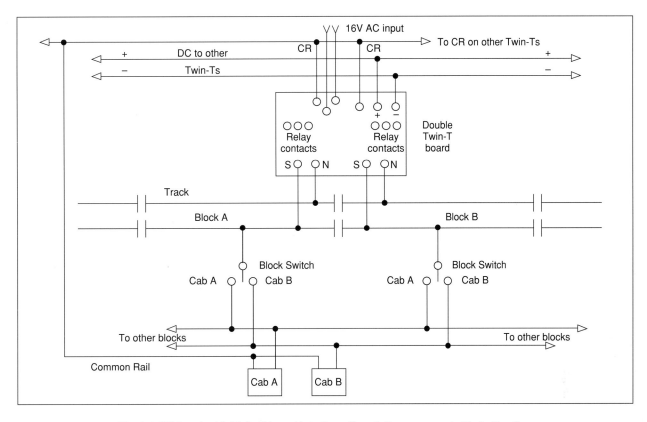

Fig. 6-2. Wiring double Twin-T board into the railroad. Gaps are needed in both rails.

cabs. The basic characteristics of the Twin-T are:

• The Twin-T detects resistance across the track in a given block. The resistance can be as high as hundreds of thousands of ohms, or it can be as low as that of a motor or a lamp.

• The Twin-T is unaffected by whether or not the throttle power is connected; train movement and direction are immaterial.

• Even if you originally used common-rail wiring, gaps are now necessary in the common rail (marked N for North in fig. 6-2) as well as in the other rail.

• Locomotives and lighted cars will trigger the Twin-T without further modification. All other cars must be equipped with a conducting wheelset and a small resistor connected across the axle.

• Dirty rails and wheels—even reasonably clean rails and wheels—will cause relays used with the Twin-T to chatter (click on and off) unless the relay coils are bypassed with large capacitors.

• Some throttles can cause the Twin-T to indicate incorrectly at certain speed settings, even though the throttle is theoretically out of the detection circle. If it happens, connect

a 1K, 1-watt resistor across the track terminals of the throttle, and use a Twin-T version that operates from a 20-volt supply.

The Double Twin-T Track Detector

It is unlikely you would use a just one Twin-T, so for this project I combined two on one PC board. The DC supply is on this board but can serve several other boards too; it is also the power supply for the relays.

The circuit of the double Twin-T is in fig. 6-3. The Twin-T detects small currents running from the CR connection (DC negative) through the base-emitter junctions of TR1 and TR2, across the N side of the track to the S side (when rolling stock is present), and back to DC positive through R1. This small current, as low as 2 milliamps in this design, turns on either TR1 or TR2, which in turn switches off TR3, de-energizing the relay. This is an unusual feature. The relay is energized when the block is empty and de-energized when rolling stock is present.

If power is connected from either throttle, the small detection current has an additional path—from CR back through the throttle, through the

block selection switch, across the track from S rail to N rail (but only if rolling stock is present), and back to CR through the base emitter junctions of TR1 and TR2 again. So either or both current paths can trigger the Twin-T into detection.

The Twin-T is powered by 16-volt AC from a separate throttle or transformer. Do not use the AC terminals of the throttle that is providing DC to the train, because there is nearly always a direct internal connection between AC and DC in the throttle. The AC is rectified and filtered to DC on the Twin-T board by diode D1 and filter capacitor C1, giving about 20 volts. This not only supplies the detection current and the power for the two relays on this board, but also for several other boards. How many depends on the relays selected, but count on ten (for a total of 20 Twin-Ts) if you use a 16VA transformer or pack as the AC source. You need only one D1 and C1 for all the boards.

When the locomotive is drawing current in the detected block, the full locomotive current passes through the base-emitter junction of TR1 or TR2. (Which transistor is affected depends on the direction of travel.) To limit the amount of current going this way, a

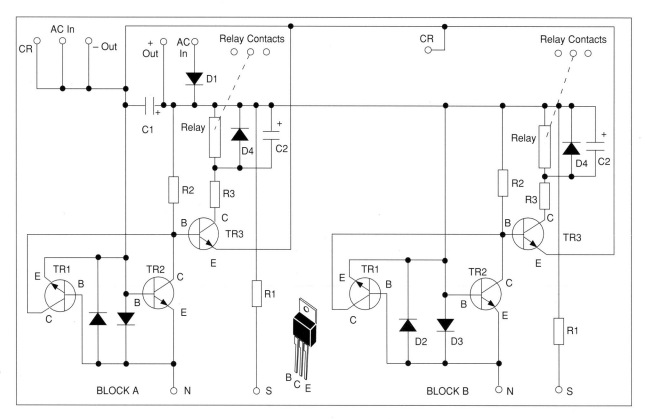

Fig. 6-3. Circuit for double Twin-T detector. Only one C1 and one D1 are required for several detector boards.

PARTS LIST FOR DOUBLE TWIN-T (FIG. 6-3)	
TR1, TR2	NPN power transistors, MJE3055T: Mouser 511-MJE3055T; Radio Shack 276-2020; Jameco 25857 (MJE3055T)
TR3	NPN power transistor, TIP31: Mouser 511-TIP31; Digi-Key TIP31GE-ND; Jameco 33048 (TIP31A)
D1, D4	Silicon diodes, 1N4004: Jameco 35991 (1N4004); Mouser 333-1N4004; Digi-Key 1N4004GI
D2, D3	Silicon diodes, 1N5404: Digi-Key 1N5404GI; Mouser 333-1N5404; Jameco 36265 (1N5404)
R1, R2	10K, 0.5-watt resistors (brown black orange)
R3	1 watt resistor, value approximately equal to relay coil resistance. Necessary only if you use a 12-volt relay; otherwise replace it with a jumper wire.
C1	1000µF, 25-volt electrolytic capacitor: Mouser (Xicon) 140-XR25V1000; Digi-Key (Panasonic) P5248
C2	220µF, 25-volt electrolytic capacitor: Mouser (Xicon) 140-XR25V220; Digi-Key (Panasonic) P5245
Relay	SPDT contacts, 24-volt coil: Digi-Key PB108-ND (Potter & Brumfield T90N5D12-24). Other relays can be used if you mount them off the PC board.
Miscellaneous	Printed circuit board 3" × 4"
	For the Double Twin-T you need two of everything except D1 and C1 (one of each).

portion of the current is bypassed through diodes D2 and D3, which are connected across the transistor junctions. This locomotive current also assists (or rather swamps) the small detector current, but diodes D2 and D3 limit the turn-on voltage for TR1 and TR2 from all sources to about 0.7 volt.

Relays

The reason for using relays is to isolate the devices they control—signals, lights, turnouts, crossing gates, train-stopping blocks—from the track current. The relays specified have 10-amp contacts. Use resistor R3 in series with the relay coil of a 12-volt relay; if

you use a 24-volt relay, omit R3 and run a wire directly from the C lead of TR3 to the coil of the relay.

Capacitor C2 eliminates most of the relay chatter by retaining energy during brief interruptions. The relays can be mounted off the PC board if that is more convenient. The relay resistance plus R3, if it is used, should be 350 to 1,000 ohms. This value is much higher than in the original Twin-T designs and reflects newer relay technology.

A 47K resistor across the rails should cause the relay to operate—or rather drop out. A resistor of this value should be connected across a conducting wheelset of every item of

rolling stock. Fig. 6-6 shows how to use small surface mount resistors, such as Digi-Key P47KE-ND or Mouser 263-47K, and conductive paint pen to do the job. You can also drill small holes in the wheels and force-fit the leads of small 0.125-watt fixed resistors (Mouser 269-47K) into them. The conductive-paint pen can be used on the inside of the wheel to ensure electrical contact.

Test your Twin-T at 47K or 56K. If it doesn't trigger, reduce the value of R1 to 8.2K. You can increase the sensitivity greatly (to about 470K) by removing D2 and D3, but do so only if you have low-current motors and power packs (Z scale and perhaps N);

otherwise TR1 and TR2 could be destroyed. You could raise the sensitivity to 2 megohms by decreasing R1, increasing R2, and removing D2 and D3; but under humid conditions enough current could leak across the ballast to trigger the Twin-T.

Assembly

Figs. 6-1 and 6-5 should provide sufficient guidance for assembling the unit. Watch for the polarities of the diodes and the capacitors, and take care that the transistors are inserted in the PC board correctly, with their metal flanges on the proper side.

To test the unit, connect the 16-volt AC and touch a 47K resistor across the N and S connections. The relay should open, then close as you remove the resistor. If nothing happens, try connecting N and S directly. If still nothing, check that your DC supply is giving 20 volts. As the two sides of the Twin-T board are substantially identical, if one side works and the other doesn't, check component polarities on the non-working side. Don't overlook the two jumper wires shown next to D and above D4 in fig. 6-5. If either is omitted, the circuit will not function.

Is there a simple detection circuit that doesn't interfere with the train power?

The Twin-T is triggered by a current flow across the track. The LOTS (Light Operated Train Sensor) system is triggered by the interruption of a beam of light or the closing of a magnetic reed switch between the rails. The light-activated sensor has a special feature compared with earlier circuits of this type—it doesn't matter if light gets between the rolling stock as the train moves past the sensors, so it is unnecessary to position the light source (usually an overhead lamp) at an angle to the sensor between the rails.

The LOTS can also be operated by reed switches between the rails. They require a magnet under the locomotive for operation, but their advantage is that they can't be triggered by changes in light level—with reed switches, for example, a hand swept over the yard does not trigger a light detector into thinking a train has moved into its orbit. So far as I know, no model railroader walks around with a handful of magnets, and the reed-switch detec-

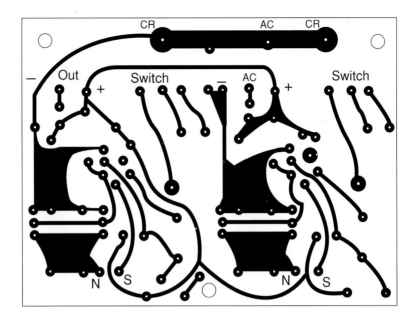

Fig. 6-4. PC board layout (copper side, full size) for double Twin-T detector.

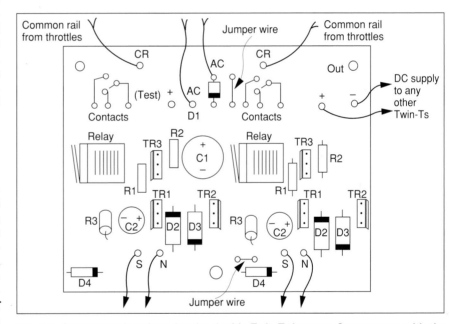

Fig. 6-5. Component locations for the double Twin-T detector. Components with the same numbers have the same values. C1 and D1 are needed only once for this or several boards.

tors are safe from enthusiastic gestures.

There are detectors that are sections of track with contacts operated by the weight of the locomotive. Avoid these for electronic circuits; one contact is invariably connected to one side of the track, creating all kinds of problems.

The LOTS light-operated train detection system

Each LOTS detector circuit is mounted on a small PC board—see fig.

6-11. On the PC board is a relay; its coil is energized when the light detector is shadowed. This is the reverse of the Twin-T, where the relay is de-energized by the presence of a train. The light detector can be either a photoconductive cell (a cadmium sulfide cell, usually shortened to CdS cell) or a photo transistor. The cell is a two-terminal device that has a low resistance when light shines on it and a high resistance when it is in the dark. The photo transistor is also usually a two-terminal device (it has no external

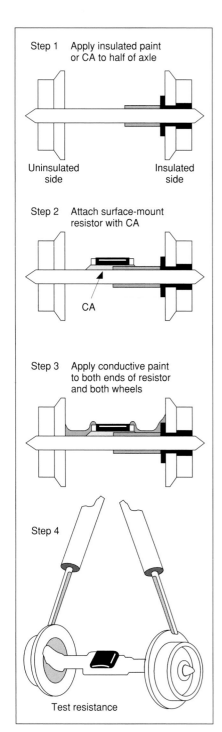

Step 1 Apply insulated paint or CA to half of axle

Uninsulated side   Insulated side

Step 2 Attach surface-mount resistor with CA

CA

Step 3 Apply conductive paint to both ends of resistor and both wheels

Step 4

Test resistance

Fig. 6-6. How to make a conductive wheelset so freight cars can be detected.

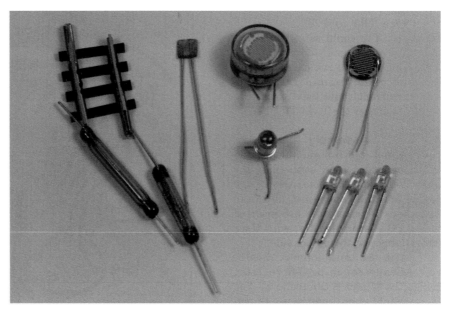

Fig. 6-7. Magnetic reed switches (left), cadmium sulfide photo cells (top center and right), and photo transistors (bottom center and right). Track is N gauge.

The relay switches are completely isolated from any other power in the layout. The LOTS board also has connections for LEDs that can be mounted on the PC board as a test indicator or installed on the control panel.

For the LOTS the "block" of occupied track is the distance between track detectors. As the train passes over each detector, the associated circuit locks into the on position. Each detector cancels all the others, as does a pair of reed switches, one at each end of the LOTS run.

As the locomotive enters or exits from a run of LOTS detectors, the reed switch closes briefly as the locomotive magnet passes over it and cancels the previous indicator. If you don't want to install magnets under your locomotives, the reed switch at each end can be replaced by the PC board of 6-12. It is the same as the LOTS board but with some components omitted. Its circuit doesn't lock on but only issues a cancel signal to the other LOTS boards. If a train is long enough that it shadows two photocells, the "track occupied" indication of the rear photocell overrides the "cancel" command of the one that has just been actuated.

The lock-and-cancel characteristic of the LOTS means that the train does not have to continuously shadow the photocell for the detector to indicate correctly. Most previous light detector circuits operated only when the train was over the photocell, or they used flip-flop transistor circuits that lost

their memory after the power was disconnected. With LOTS, the first shadowing of the light detector or photo transistor says, "the block is occupied" to the circuit; and the block stays "occupied," no matter how many more shadows and light bursts flash past the detector, until the next light detector is shadowed. There is no need to carefully misalign light source and light detector to avoid strips of light between boxcars as they pass over the detector.

What light to use

The CdS cells and photo transistors specified work from tungsten filament light (conventional light bulbs) or daylight. Overhead incandescents or fluorescents may be sufficient, but most detectors require a booster light, such as a grain-of-wheat lamp over the track. LEDs aren't sufficient for that purpose.

How LOTS works

If the photocell is lit, its resistance is low, which keeps TR1 from conducting. If the photocell is shadowed, its resistance goes up; TR1 is switched on and in turn switches on TR3. The relay coil is energized and TR2 is latched on by the voltage now at the junction of R3 and R4. Now even if the light detector is out of the shadow, TR1 can't turn off because it's in lock-step with TR2. The only way TR1 and TR2 can switch off is if a cancel voltage appears across R7 that is higher than the latch voltage on TR2. This

base connection) that conducts when light shines on its lens or surface. Either can be used for the LOTS. The photo transistor is smaller than the CdS cell but is fussy about the positioning of the triggering light because of its smaller surface area.

In the same way as the Twin-T, the relay can be used to control devices like signals and crossing gates.

Fig. 6-8. The LOTS (Light Operated Train Sensor) is electrically independent of the track and can be integrated with any layout. It can be used with command control or sound systems. When shadowed by a train, each photo detector indicates a section of track in use and cancels all others automatically.

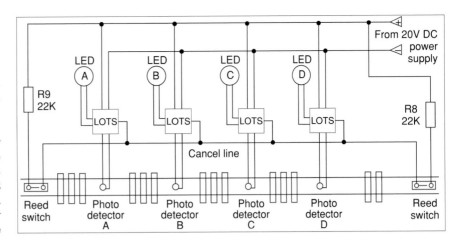

cancel voltage appears whenever another detector is activated. With no detector activated the cancel voltage is close to zero. With one activated it rises to just under 1 volt; the instant a second one is activated it momentarily goes higher (over 1.25 volts) until the first is off.

The voltage drop across the CdS cell should be about 0.5 volt shadowed and 0.15 volt in bright light. If a photo transistor is used the voltages are about 4 shadowed and 0.3 in bright light.

The power supply is identical to the simple rectifier-capacitor unit in fig. 5-4 of Chapter 5. It can power up to a dozen LOTS boards. If you use photo transistors, you may find that the relay gets energized even in bright light. Reducing the power supply voltage should correct this. The easiest way to reduce the DC voltage is to connect the power supply board to 12 or 12.6 volts AC instead of 16. Changing the relay voltage is no help in this case—a 24-volt coil will still energize at 14 volts.

Fig. 6-9. (Right) The LOTS circuit.

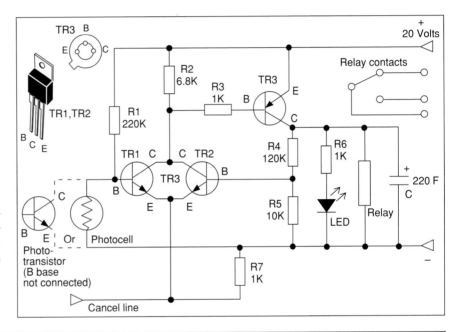

PARTS LIST FOR LOTS DETECTION SYSTEM (FIGS. 6-9 and 6-12)

TR1, TR2	NPN power transistors, TIP29: Mouser 511-TIP29; Digi-Key TIP29GE-ND; Jameco 33021 (TIP29A)
TR3	PNP small signal transistor, 2N2905: Digi-Key 2N2905; Mouser 511-2N2905
C	220µF, 25-volt electrolytic capacitor: Mouser (Xicon) 140-XR25V220; Digi-Key (Panasonic) P5245
Relay	SPDT (1 Form C), 24 volt, 1,440-ohm coil: Digi-Key Z732-ND (Omron G5L-114P-PS-DC24)
LED	Any type
R1	220K, 0.25-watt resistor (red red yellow). Omitted from the PC board when reed switches are used as detectors, but in that case you will need one of these for each reed switch.
R2	6.8K, 0.25-watt resistor (red gray red)
R3, R6, R7	1.0K, 0.5-watt resistor (brown black red). R7 is used on only one LOTS board.
R4	120K, 0.25-watt resistor (brown red yellow)
R5	10K, 0.25-watt resistor (brown black orange)
R8, R9	22K, 0.25-watt resistors (red red orange)
R10	150K, 0.25-watt resistor (brown green yellow). You need this only if you use photocells at the ends of the run.
R11	18K, 0.25-watt resistor (brown gray orange). You need this only if you use photocells at the ends of the run.
R12	82K, 0.25-watt resistor (gray red orange). You need these only if you use reed switches as detectors.
CdS cells or	Photoconductive cell, maximum 3K lit, minimum 20K in shadow: Mouser 338-54C348; EG&G Vactec VT-811 or VT-701
Phototransistors	30-volt NPN type, L14G2: Mouser 570-L14G2; Digi-Key (Panasonic) PN168PA. The E connection is closest to the lug on the case; the C connection is farthest from it. If there is an extra connection between the E and C, do not use it.
or Reed switches	Miniature types, SPST normally open, no special ratings: Hamlin MDSR-4-.104 or MDRR-4-.104; Hasco ORD-211 or ORD-221
Miscellaneous	PC board material 2" × 2¼", one for each LOTS unit
	Alnico magnets, not plastic, one per locomotive: Radio Shack 64-1880; Edmund Scientific D38,685

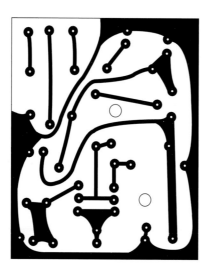

Fig. 6-10. LOTS PC board layout, full size, and component locations.

The parts list calls for Omron 24-volt relays. They have contact ratings of 5 amps and have a high coil resistance of over 1,400 ohms. I don't advise substitution unless the alternate has a similarly high coil resistance.

Assembly

Note carefully the positions of the metal sides of TR1 and TR2 when you fit them to the PC board, and watch for the metal tab at the side of TR3. Be sure to observe the polarities of capacitor C and the LED. Mounting the LED on the control panel instead of the PC board is a simple matter of extending a pair of wires. TR2, C, and the LED are not used on the cancel-only board (fig. 6-13).

All the PC boards have a cancel connection, and all of them should be joined. Only one cancel resistance (R7) is necessary for the system, so only one board needs to have R7 fitted; it doesn't matter which. The other boards have nothing connected in its place.

You can wire the CdS cell either way to the C and E connections on the board, but you must connect the collector of the photo transistor to C and its

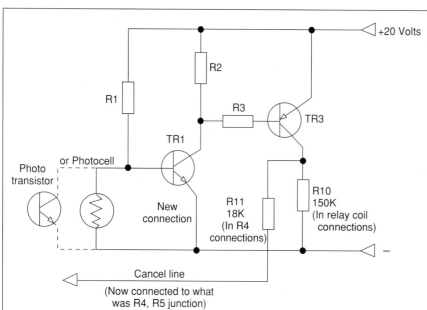

Fig. 6-11. LOTS boards with latching components inserted (left) and without (right). Boards without latches are required at the end of a LOTS run if reeds are not used as cancel switches.

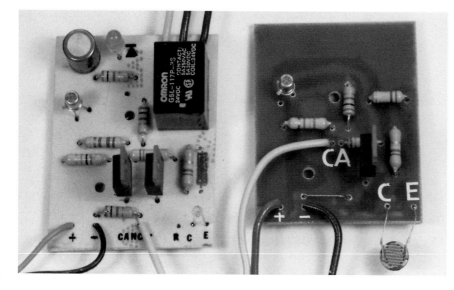

Fig. 6-12. If an all-optical LOTS system is preferred, then this modified non-latching LOTD circuit can replace the reed switches, R8, and R9 in Fig. 6-8.

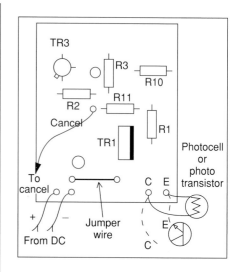

Fig. 6-13. Component locations for the circuit of Fig. 6-12. The PC board is the same as fig. 6-10. Components not identified are omitted from this board.

emitter to E. The shorter of the two leads of a two-lead photo transistor is the collector. Mount the photocell or photo transistor close to its LOTS board; it must, of course, be above the layout.

The positive and negative DC connections go directly to the power supply. Because of the high resistance of the relay coil there should be no interference between boards. If you do get any erratic jitter of the relays, try a 100µF 25-volt electrolytic capacitor between the positive and negative DC connections on each board.

Reed switches as detectors

You can also use magnetic reed switches to trigger the same LOTS circuit. These switches detect only locomotives and cars fitted with magnets. Fig. 6-15 shows a magnet cemented under an HO locomotive. Remember that the magnet cannot hang down below rail level.

Fig. 6-16 shows how each reed switch is wired into the system. There are two modifications to the PC board. Resistor R1 (220K, between C and DC positive) is omitted from the board and wired in series with the reed switch. Resistor R12 (82K) is added between C and DC negative. The location of R12 is shown dotted in fig. 6-10. The reed switch connects to the LOTS board only at connection C. Its other connection is via a 220K resistor to DC plus, as shown in fig. 6-16.

Remember, you must position reed switches so that the flat side of the internal switch blades, not the edge, faces the magnet. Don't confuse reed switches with reed relays. A reed relay consists of one or more reed switches inside a coil. Current through the coil magnetizes the reed switches. Directional detection is possible with reed switches if you place them off-center between the rails.

Can Hall Effect devices be used as detectors?

These transistor-like devices are semiconductor switches in small plastic cases. Much like reed switches, they are triggered when a magnet passes over them. The magnet is more critical than for a reed switch and

Fig. 6-16. Reed switches can replace photocells or photo transistors as LOTS detectors. The text explains the necessary change in resistor values.

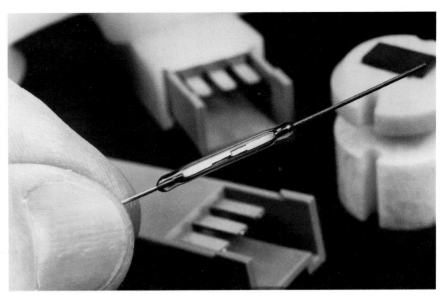

Fig. 6-14. Magnetically operated reed switches can be less than 0.6" in length, ideal for location between tracks. Photo from Wabash Magnetics.

Fig. 6-15. A disk magnet fitted under an HO diesel loco. Magnets from Edmund Scientific are ⅛" thick. Thicker ones must usually be recessed.

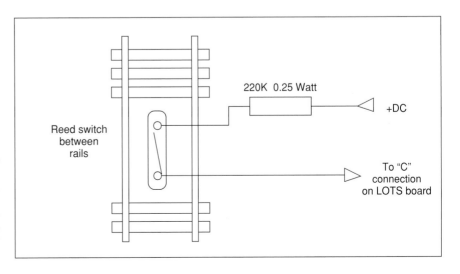

Reed switch between rails

220K 0.25 Watt

+DC

To "C" connection on LOTS board

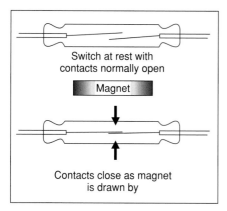

Fig. 6-17. The normally open contacts of a magnetic reed switch close in a magnetic field. The distance between the magnet and the reed depends on magnet strength.

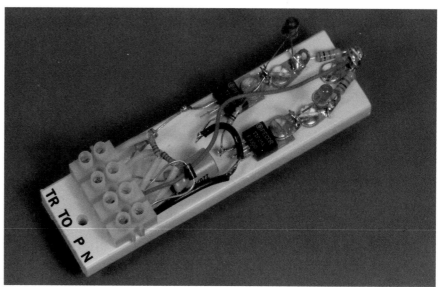

Fig. 6-18. The block-in-use detector can be assembled on a plastic base.

must be polarized so that a specific pole passes over the device. Hall-Effect devices appear to have no real advantage over reed switches.

Is a block-in-use indicator simpler than a train detector?

A block-in-use detector indicates both power connected to the block and the presence of rolling stock. Simply indicating that power is connected to the block is just a matter of connecting a panel light to an extra pair of contacts on the block selector switches. It could be powered from the throttle, but if you don't want it to dim or go out at low speed, you need a separate fixed power supply for the lamp. However, if the presence of rolling stock must also be indicated, an electronic circuit is necessary.

The circuit is shown in fig. 6-18. The power supply is again the 20-volt DC supply of fig. 5-4, which can supply up to twenty of these block-in-use circuits, but the 16-volt AC source for the 20-volt DC supply must be completely separate from any power pack running the trains. Common rail wiring is okay; the blocks detected will have gaps in one rail.

Just as with the Twin-T, resistors are needed across the axle of a conducting wheelset for each item of rolling stock (except locomotives and lighted cars). The circuit is simpler and doesn't need a printed circuit board. It can also be used as a signal system. When the track is clear, and no throttle is connected, TR2 conducts and turns on green LEDs (two or three may be connected in series). When the track is occupied or the throttle is con-

PARTS LIST FOR BLOCK-IN-USE DETECTOR (FIG. 6-18)	
R1, R2	2.2K, 0.25-watt resistors (red red red)
R3, R4	1K, 0.25-watt resistors (brown black red)
R5	10K, 0.25-watt resistor (brown black orange)
C	220µF, 25-volt electrolytic capacitor: Mouser (Xicon) 140-XR25V220; Digi-Key (Panasonic) P5245
TR1, TR2	NPN power transistors, TIP29: Mouser 511-TIP29; Digi-Key TIP29GE-ND; Jameco 33021 (TIP29A)
D	Silicon rectifier diode, 1N4004: Digi-Key 1N4004GI; Mouser 333-1N4004; Radio Shack 276-1103
Miscellaneous	Four-terminal strip (Radio Shack 274-678)
	Five each solder lugs or solderless ring tongues, 6-32 screws, and nuts
	LEDs, any type rated 20 milliamps or more
	1.25" × 4.5" piece of plastic or wood for base

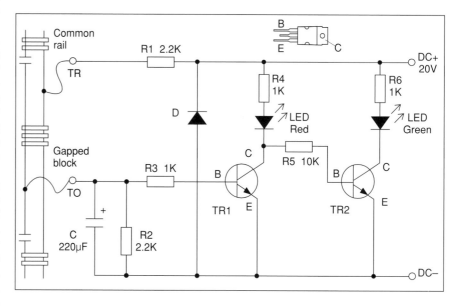

Fig. 6-19. The block-in-use detector indicates if the throttle is connected to a block as well as detecting locomotives and cars fitted with a conductive wheel set.

Fig. 6-20. (Right) Wiring the block-in-use detector.

Fig. 6-21. (Below right) The tunnel tracker: LEDs at the control panel indicate a train traversing hidden tracks.

nected, TR1 conducts, turns off TR2 and the green lights, and turns on its own red LEDs. If required, 24-volt relays like those specified for the LOTS system could replace the LEDs in either transistor collector circuit.

Resistor R2 and diode D protect the circuit from high track voltage. Capacitor C provides some hysteresis or delay so the lights don't flicker if the wheels are dirty.

Connect 15K resistors across one pair of conducting wheels on each car. For small scales use a surface-mount resistor such as Mouser P15KE-ND. For larger scales (and axles) you can use conventional use 0.125- or 0.25-watt resistors. As with the Twin-T, no resistors are needed for powered locomotives or lighted rolling stock.

The block-in-use detector is not as sensitive as the Twin-T (it detects a 15K resistance compared with 47K), but it offers the advantage of a simple signal system. The block in use can have red LEDs at each end when occupied, then green LEDs as the train moves out of the block. Other LEDs can be connected in series and mounted on the control panel.

Wiring the Block-in-Use Detector

Fig. 6-18 is a photo of the unit, and fig. 6-20 is a wiring diagram. Assemble the unit on a piece of wood, hardboard, or heavy plastic—I used a piece of plastic edge trim material from a building supply store. Be careful with the polarity for diode D, capacitor C, and the LEDs. The center pins, the collector leads of TR1 and TR2, are clipped short, and the C connections are made through solder tags under the metal flanges of these transistors. (The flange is also a collector connection for these devices; cutting the center pin reduces the chance of short circuits for sloppy assemblers!) The photo shows the LEDs on the board; you can place them wherever you like. Secure the terminal strip and capacitor with silicone sealant; use machine screws and nuts to hold the transistors in place.

I labeled the four terminals of my unit P and N for positive and negative DC power input, TR for the common

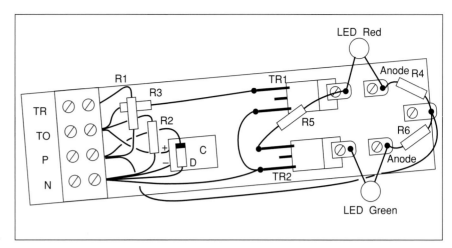

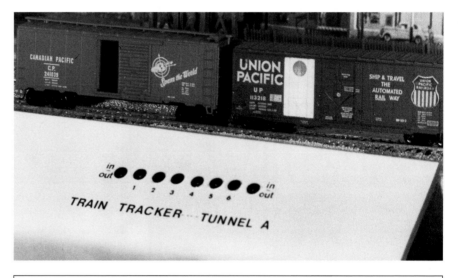

PARTS LIST FOR TUNNEL TRACKER (FIG. 6-21)

U1, U2	CMOS ICs, hex inverting buffers, 4049 or 4009: Mouser 511-4049 or 511-4009; Digi-Key CD4049UBE or CD4009CN
U3	CMOS IC, quadruple 2-input AND gate 4081: Mouser 511-4081; Digi-Key CD4081BCN
U4, U5	TTL ICs, BCD to decimal decoder/driver, 74LS45: Digi-Key DM7445N; Newark SN74LS145N; Mouser 511-74LS42. (The 74LS42, 74LS45 and 74LS145 can all be used. The -42 must be used only with LEDs; the -45 and -145 are preferred. Either can be used with higher currents than just the LEDs and would be useful if relays replace the LEDs.)
BR	100-volt bridge rectifier: Mouser 333-BR32; Digi-Key PB61-ND
TTR	5-volt positive three-terminal regulator 7805: Digi-Key AN7805; Mouser 511-L7805CV
C1 to C8	0.01µF, 100-volt film capacitors: Digi-Key (Panasonic) EF1103; Mouser (Xicon) 23AB310
C9	100µF, 10-volt electrolytic capacitor: Digi-Key (Panasonic) P5634; Mouser (Xicon) 140-XR10V100
C10	1,000µF, 10-volt electrolytic capacitor: Digi-Key (Panasonic) P5642; Mouser (Xicon) 140-XR10V1000
R1, R2	220K, 0.25-watt resistors (red red yellow)
R3 to R8	10K, 0.25-watt resistors (brown black orange)
Miscellaneous	PC board material 4" × 5" IC socket (14 pin, one): Mouser 506-214-AG39D; Digi-Key AE8914 IC sockets (16 pin, four): Mouser 506-216-AG39D; Digi-Key AE8916
Power supply	Mouser 41FD300 is a 6.3-volt, 0.3-amp transformer. Cord, fuse, and on-off switch are needed as in the FPW throttle of Chapter 4. You can use a tinplate power transformer as described in the text, or a wall transformer. Or use either of the following DC output items and connect them directly to the TTR input and negative (in correct polarity, of course): Digi-Key T410-ND; Mouser 41AC114 (both 9 volts DC, 200 milliamps). Components BR and C10 can then be omitted.

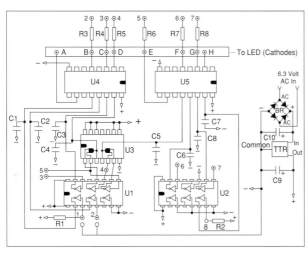

Fig. 6-22. Tunnel tracker circuit

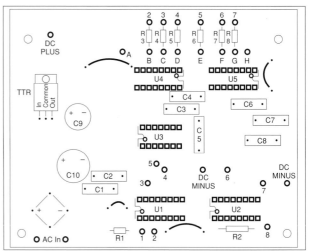

Fig. 6-23. Component layout for the tunnel tracker. Note the four jumper wires. Not shown are the six wires visible in fig. 6-26 joining pairs of points numbered 2 through 7.

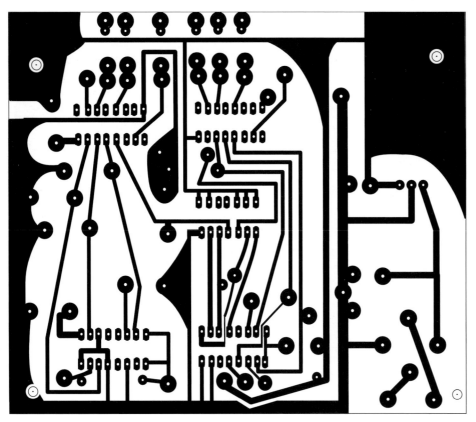

Fig. 6-24. Full-size PC board layout for the tunnel tracker.

rail track connection, and TO for the other track connection. The block-in-use detector is relatively foolproof. Should both LEDs turn on together, reduce R5 to 4.7k. Should neither turn on, check the polarity of C and D.

How can I tell where a train is in a long tunnel or concealed helix?

I used a Tunnel Tracker for a year on my layout. It was useful for locat-ing where the train had derailed, so I knew exactly where to crawl in the darkness to worry it back onto track. I eventually became frustrated and removed the tunnel but kept the circuit!

The Tunnel Tracker

This circuit has a display of eight LEDs on the control panel (see fig. 6-21). The LEDs at each end flash briefly as a train enters or exits the tunnel (or whatever stretch of track it is installed on). While it is in the tunnel, six LEDs follow the passage of the train past six detectors. The circuit is bi-direc-tional; the LEDs will track either direction.

Reed switches are used as detectors, so the locomotives must be fitted with small actuat-ing magnets. The tunnel tracker is completely independent of propulsion power and uses no track circuitry.

Fig. 6-22 shows the circuit. U4 and U5 are logic-coding inte-grated circuits, binary-coded-deci-mal to decimal converters. They are not used as such here, but each IC contains four switches. Each switch, when turned on by an external trigger, will keep the other three off. These eight switches are connected to pins labeled A through H at the top of the board. Each switch is rated at 30 volts and 80 milliamps, but in this circuit they are used only to switch an LED each at 5 volts and 20 milliamps.

Integrated circuit U3, a quad 2-input AND gate, is used to connect the switches of U4 and U5 so that the last switch of U4 is turned off by the first switch of U5 and vice versa. This links the two sets of four switches to give a total of eight, any one of which when turned on will turn off all the others.

Eight magnetic reed switches turn on the eight IC switches. The six IC switches in the middle are locked on as soon as the associated reed switch is closed. This is done with resistors R3 through R8, which connect the output switch connections to the input reed switches on pins 2 through 7. There are no latching resistors for the reed switches at pins 1 and 8; if there were, the exit LED would stay on, as there is no corresponding canceling signal after the train has passed the last reed switch. The LEDs corresponding to pins 1 and 8 are those at pins A and H, and they flash only momentarily as the train enters or leaves. U1 and U2 are hex inverter gates. They function only to make the latching function polarity correct.

Capacitors C1 through C8 suppress electrical interference from brush sparking and switch-machine pushbutton arcing; the interference can cause false triggering.

The input required is 6.3 volts AC at 0.5 amps or more, from a separate transformer. The printed circuit board contains the rectifier, filter capacitor, and a 5-volt three terminal regulator (TTR). The ICs, LEDs, and the reed relay line are all supplied from the resulting stabilized 5-volt supply. The TTR will accept up to about 8.5 volts AC, if you want to use a Lionel or American Flyer transformer set to minimum speed. No component changes are required.

Assembly

This is a board of substantial size, but there are not too many components. Polarity is critical for everything but the resistors and capacitors C1-C8. Be extra careful with the ICs, because two of them (the 74LS45s) are "upside down" in their pin locations compared to the others.

The board should have the shortest connecting wires at the reed switch end. The wire length to the control panel of the LEDs and each associated 150-ohm resistor is not critical—in other words, locate the board near the tunnel, not near the control panel.

Static electricity can destroy the ICs U1, U2, and U3. Do not remove them from the tube or the pink or black plastic they were packed in until you

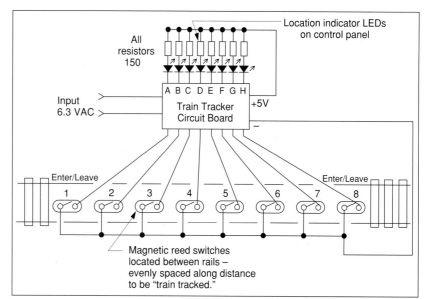

Fig. 6-25. Connecting the tunnel tracker to the layout and the control panel.

Fig. 6-26. The tunnel tracker board.

are ready to insert them in the board. Insert them last, along with ICs U4 and U5, which are not quite so fussy. It's a good idea to ensure that you are not charged with static before picking them up. Touch a cold-water faucet first—plumbing is nearly always grounded. If your pipes are plastic, go back to the water meter! (Factory workers who assemble equipment with these ICs are always grounded through a wrist strap, and the workroom floors have conductive paint or tiles.)

Note the location of the four wire jumpers at the top of the board. They are identified in fig. 6-23 and visible in fig. 6-26.

7 Sound on the Railroad

Figure 7-1. Sound can appear to come from industrial buildings. This 4" speaker is located in the base of a building, and recorded sound is directed to it.

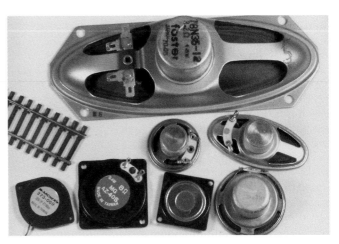

Fig. 7-2. A selection of speakers for on-board and around-the-layout sound. The smallest is 1¼" diameter and the largest is 3" × 5". The track section is HO gauge.

TRAINS ARE mechanical objects. They make noise—lots of noise if you're close at hand. Models aren't as noisy, but electronic circuits to reproduce steam and diesel engine noise have been around for some time; and recently they've been augmented by mooing cows, gobbling turkeys and neighing horses, all courtesy of electronics.

Many designs for electronic sound circuits have been published, but most of the devices they rely on are obsolete. Many designs required the use of custom integrated circuits that were originally made for toys. Finding the specified ICs after a couple of years have passed is impossible.

Is there an easy way to add sound to the layout?

The easiest way, and to my mind one of the most effective, is to record locomotive, railroad crossing, yard, or factory sounds and route them to the appropriate parts of the scale town (or countryside). Loudspeakers small enough to fit inside N or HO buildings are available, some for as little as a

dollar. Fig. 7-2 shows a selection, ranging from 1¼" in diameter up to 3" × 5". They are rated at 0.1 watt—they are not 100-watt (and $100-and-up) bass reflex units.

Fig. 7-3 illustrates how the output of a cassette tape player can be switched around the layout to several small speakers. Normally the output comes from the headphone jack, which switches off the internal speaker. The power from the headphone jack is insufficient to drive a speaker (it is internally reduced from the available internal speaker power so that it won't blow your ears off with acid rock), so it's necessary to add a small amplifier—200 milliwatts is sufficient. Radio Shack 277-1008 is such a unit; it has an internal speaker. Disconnect its two speaker leads, and connect one to the selector contact of the rotary switch and the other to one terminal of all the speakers around the layout. Connect the other terminals of those speakers to terminals of the rotary switch. You will need to add a 47-ohm, 0.5-watt resistor to the headphone output to protect the internal circuits of

the recorder in case it plays with neither headphones nor external speaker connected.

In most cases the volume available from the cassette player will be sufficient. If your layout is large, you may need a high-power amplifier, but be careful not to blow out speaker cones with high power—keep the volume control low.

Speakers need a barrier or baffle so that sound from the back of the cone won't cancel sound from the front. Locating the speaker in the floor of a factory building (see fig. 7-1) works well. The baseboard of the layout is also good, but place a fabric screen across the cone opening to keep dust, grime, and plaster rocks out of the cone (and also conceal the speaker).

Can I really get good sound out of such small speakers? Don't I need woofers and tweeters?

Scale sound is difficult to define unless you've experienced it. Imagine your layout is a real railroad and you're standing on a hill a quarter mile away. Most low-frequency sound dissipates before it reaches you; what you hear are the higher frequencies. One-fifth of a watt of power into a 3" or 4" speaker will sound just about right. Speaker efficiency also plays a part—small speakers are designed to be efficient because they are for use with low powers.

Smaller speakers are directional—there's no doubt where they are located. On a layout, though, we want the sound to come from a specific source; we aren't looking for high-quality, low-distortion, wide-dispersion, concert-hall-quality sound reproduction.

What about sounds from toys?

Round about Santa-time each year the department stores and the discount toy stores offer train sets and toy trains that make most modelers take one look, shudder, and keep going. Next time stop long enough to check if there is a sound unit—the package may say "Whistle, bell, and choo-choo sounds!" (even if it's a diesel).

The sound unit shown in figs. 7-4 and 7-5 was inside a plastic station building, which I simply considered part of the packaging. I added a separate battery pack, which holds two AA cells. The sound unit has pushbuttons that yield two horn blasts, about twenty steam chuffs, and sixteen bell chimes in succession. The speaker is 2" in diameter and will fit in any O or G scale locomotive.

This sound unit is typical. The push-button contacts can be seen from the back of the PC board in the form of four circle-and-dot copper traces. They are contacted by conductive rubber disks sandwiched between the copper and the plastic button. These disks read about 100 ohms, so a 100-ohm resistor connected across any of the contact pairs will make the unit sound.

Thus we have available an (almost) incredibly simple sound system. Magnetic reed switches between the rails can be connected to the push-button contacts. As the locomotive passes, the magnet closes the contact and out comes the sound. For example, four reed switches could be arranged to produce two horn blasts followed by bells and two more horn blasts.

If a train position detector is used (such as the Twin-T in Chapter 6), the relay contact of the detector will stay closed over a given block of track; the steam chuff—or bell or horn—will then be continuous. See fig. 7-6.

Keep the entire sound module close to the trigger points (the reed switches). The unit is sensitive to static electricity—don't touch parts without grounding yourself first, and use a grounded soldering iron, if possible.

Why are integrated circuits for sound, such as the SN76487N and the SN76488N, no longer available?

These ICs were among the first digital sound circuits. They generated hiss, or white noise, and had as many as three oscillators for sounds and

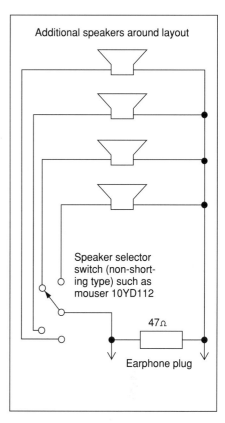

Fig. 7-3. Switching sound from a cassette player around the layout.

interruptions. Packaging was their advantage to the hobbyist; a complex sound system could be made with just one plug-in IC. Packaging was also the cause of their demise, since packaging is often 80 percent of the cost of manufacture.

In the current trend, "chip on board," the bare chip without the package is bonded to the PC board. One can be seen as the dark area at

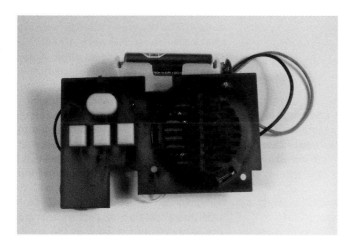

Fig. 7-4. A toy sound unit removed from its station. Train sets sometimes contain battery-operated devices for horn, bell, and chuff such as this.

Fig. 7-5. Rear view of the toy sound unit. The pushbutton contacts can be seen through the board. They can be replaced by reed switches between the rails for automatic crossing whistles and bells.

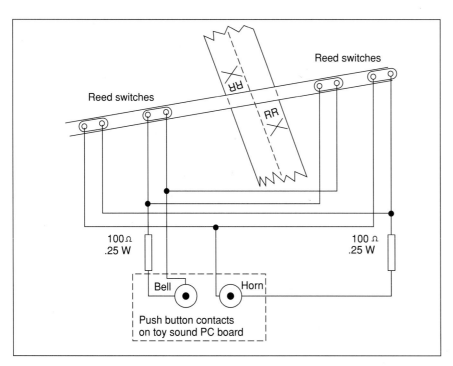

Fig. 7-6. Toy sound unit with added wiring to sound automatically at highway crossings.

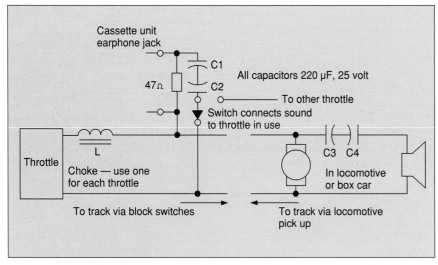

Fig. 7-7. Sending sound through the rails requires choke to keep sound out of the throttle, and blocking capacitors to keep the DC train power out of the cassette and speaker.

the lower right of the PC board in fig. 7-5. This type of assembly is impossible for the hobbyist, and the manufacturers of the chips for obvious reasons will supply the bare chips only to toy makers and only in large quantities. A tiny, unpackaged, bare chip is simply not an off-the-shelf item.

Another option is the programmable digital IC. These are special devices in normal packages that can have high-quality sound installed digitally. They have built-in memory to retain the sound; the greater the memory, the greater the duration of the sound. Although these blank ICs are readily available, the equipment to program them is not—in the future it may be.

How can sound be sent through the rails to a speaker in the locomotive?

Sound can be piggybacked onto filtered DC throttle output. Fig. 7-7 shows the requirements. Use essentially the same sound sources as the ones suggested above to direct sound around the layout, with a small speaker located in the locomotive or tender. The requirements are:

• Choke coils wired in series with at least one throttle lead. With some reverse loop wiring and the use of common rail, it's advisable to have chokes in both throttle leads (fig. 7-7 shows only one). The chokes keep the throttle from shorting out the sound signals, which are AC voltages between 50 and 5,000 Hertz.

• Capacitors in one lead from the amplifier and in one lead of the speaker in the locomotive. These must be bipolar electrolytic types (or two separate polarized types wired back to back, as shown in fig. 7-7). These capacitors keep DC from the throttle from damaging the amplifier and the speaker while letting the sound AC voltages through.

• Filtered DC throttles. Pulse throttles (all commercial DC throttles are pulse types) contain 60- or 120-Hertz pulses. These unavoidably cause the speaker to rattle, spoiling the sound.

Suitable bipolar electrolytic capacitors (also referred to as non-polarized) are Mouser (Xicon) 140-BPR50V100 (100μF, 50 volts) and Digi-Key (Panasonic) P1129 (100μF, 25 volts). Each bipolar can be replaced by two conventional polarized electrolytics of twice the capacity (220μF), wired as in fig. 7-7.

The choke coils are more difficult. They must be high inductance and low resistance. A low resistance is necessary because the motor DC current runs through them. A 1-ohm coil resistance would drop 1 volt with a 1 amp motor. The woofer coil from Radio Shack Crossover Network 40-8425 is suitable. The choke from their Noise Eliminator kit 270-030 is also suitable and costs less.

The speaker you use is limited by the space available in the tender or diesel shell. Fig. 7-17 shows holes in the bottom of an HO brass tender (it came from the manufacturer that way) to permit a speaker to direct the sound down toward the track. For the smaller scales you'll have to drill your own holes. A wad of cotton batting wrapped around the back of the small speaker helps sound quality. In the larger scales sound can be improved by using a larger speaker (2" for O scale, 2½" for G) and directing the sound upward, but you'll need to devise a way to get the sound through the coal.

What is needed for steam sound on board?

On-board sound implies not only small speakers but small circuits. Mostly these sound circuits are for steam locomotives, giving speed-sensitive rates of chuff. Such hiss (white noise) circuits aren't easily made; the devices in them must be selected carefully. I've never made one work to my complete satisfaction.

Fig. 7-8 shows a circuit formerly used by Lionel. It consists of a noise (steam hiss) generator, an amplifier powered from the track voltage, and an interrupter switch driven by the tip of a piston rod. The noise generator is a reverse-connected transistor with the collector disconnected (it's the far left transistor in the circuit). The circuit works on AC (and works well) and is designed for Lionel's 8.5-volt minimum track voltage.

What are good noise sources for steam and whistle sounds?

The non-collector-connection transistor and the germanium diode as noise sources are non-starters, because you may have to test 50 of them to find one that is noisy, and in any event the germanium diode is obsolete and all but unavailable.

The Zener diode circuit shown in fig. 7-11 is a consistent noise producer but requires at least 12 volts to operate properly; it won't work satisfactorily from a 9-volt battery. Its output is lower than the three-IC circuit below, even if the latter is working at low voltage. The Zener diode circuit works better for sound-through-the-rails or around-the-layout uses than for on-board sound.

There are (or were) available two small ICs, National Semiconductor MM5837N and MM5437N, that produce "pseudo-random" digital noise. At the time of writing the MM5437N is still available. Fig. 7-10 shows how to wire it as a noise generator. "Pseudo-random" means it's a gimmick method of making something that sounds like the noise from your TV when the station goes off the air.

Fig. 7-10 also shows a three-IC circuit that does practically the same thing but uses standard off-the-shelf ICs. The PC board layout and component locations are in Fig. 7-15. This

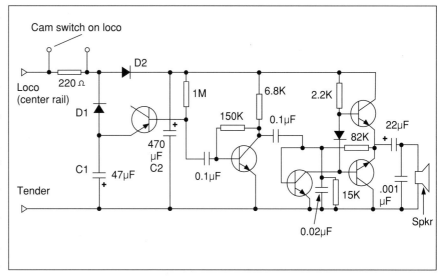

Fig. 7-8. This steam chuff circuit was formerly used in some Lionel steam locomotives. AC track power offers an advantage in that simple circuits can be powered from the track .

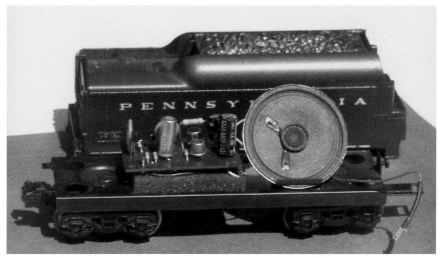

Fig. 7-9. A steam sound unit mounted in a Lionel tender.

circuit generates continuous steam-like sound when powered by a 5- to 12-volt supply—a 9-volt battery on board is recommended. To use the circuit to generate synchronized chuffs, a small IC amplifier is needed to drive the speaker, plus a switch to interrupt the amplifier once or twice per drive wheel revolution. The whole affair can be crammed into an HO boxcar; O and G scales have plenty of room.

Because the noise output differs with the two noise circuits there are adjustments to component values in the amplifier part of the circuit. These are indicated in the parts lists.

Assembly

The three-IC noise generator uses CMOS integrated circuits, so insert them last and take care to avoid dam-

aging them with static electricity—see the precautions described at the end of Chapter 6. Observe the position of terminal 1 of the ICs; it is indicated on both the upper and lower board diagrams. Be careful that you connect C3 with the correct polarity, and don't overlook the six jumper wires on the board.

You can assemble the Zener noise generator (fig. 7-11) on terminal or tag strips. No special precautions about static electricity are needed, but watch the polarity of ZD and the two electrolytic capacitors. The connections of TR are, viewed from the bottom, B in the center (connected to ZD), E adjacent to the lug on the case (connected to the negative side of the power supply), and C, which is farthest from the lug on the case.

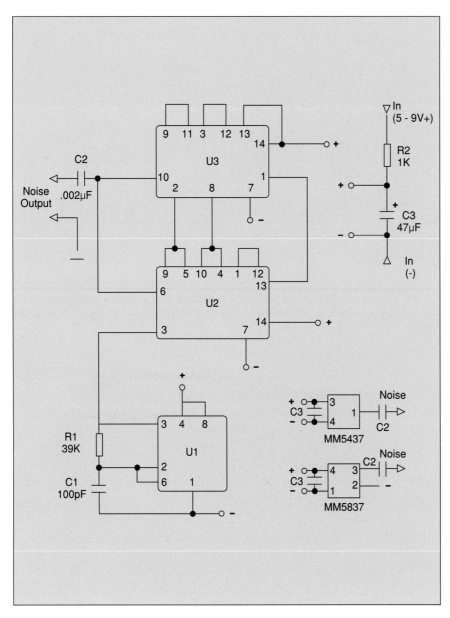

Fig. 7-10. Steam hiss noise generation using integrated circuits. The two single ICs shown in the inset are in short supply. The three-IC circuit uses ordinary ICs.

PARTS LISTS FOR THREE-IC NOISE GENERATOR (FIGS. 7-10)

U1	CMOS timer IC: Mouser 570-CA555CE; Digi-Key LM555CN; Radio Shack 276-1718
U2	4006 18-bit static shift register IC: Mouser 511-4006; Digi-Key CD4006BCN
U3	4030 quad exclusive OR gate IC: Mouser 511-4030; Digi-Key CD4030BE
R1	39K, 0.25-watt resistor (orange white orange)
R2	1K, 0.25-watt resistor (brown black red). This resistor is mounted between the PC board positive terminal and the positive terminal of the battery.
C1	100 picofarad (pF), 5% precision type capacitor rated at 50 volts or more: Mouser 140-CA50S101J; Digi-Key P4024
C2	2,200pF, 100-volt ceramic-disk or miniature film-type capacitor: Mouser 140-PM2A223K; Digi-Key P4189
C3	47µF, 16-volt electrolytic capacitor: Mouser 140-XR16V47; Digi-Key P6331
Miscellaneous	Two 14-pin IC sockets: Mouser 506-214-AG29D; Digi-Key A9214 One 8-pin IC socket: Mouser 506-208-AG29D; Digi-Key A9208 PC board material 1" × 1⅞"

Amplifier

An amplifier for on-board or through-the-rails sound is shown in fig. 7-12, with PC board layout and component locations in fig. 7-16. This can be driven by either of the two noise generators just described or by the MM5437N integrated circuit. It is the second element of steam sound, with the interrupter to be described next.

The amplifier works on 6 to 12 volts DC. Because both the amplifier and the noise generators draw small currents (the noise generator draws less than 2 milliamps and the amplifier draws according to sound level) I've specified an on-board 9-volt battery for the power source. The output power of the amplifier is 1 watt, more than adequate for speakers of 1" to 3" diameter.

If you use it for through-the-rails sound, the same 9-volt battery supply can be retained if the noise source is the MM5437N or the three-IC sound board. The Zener diode noise circuit needs more than 9 volts, so it can't be used on board. For through-the-rails it needs a separate DC supply, such as the 22-volt supply specified in Chapter 5 for CD units.

The LM386-N4 IC used can have its amplification changed externally without the need for a volume control. The changes depend on the sound source you select:
- Zener noise—maximum amplification needed
    insert C4 into the PC board
    wire a jumper across location holes of R4
    R3 should be 10K
    omit MM5437N and its socket; also omit CX2, C6, and R2
- MM5437N—medium amplification needed
    use CX1 and CX2
    R3 should be 82K
    omit C4 and R4
- Three-IC noise circuit— low amplification needed
    R3 should be 1 megohm
    omit MM5437N and socket, also omit CX1, CX2, C4, and R4

If the noise is harsh (with popcorn crackles superimposed, for instance), the LM386N-4 is being overdriven; double the value of R3. If the sound level is too low, insert C4 and R4; if it is still too low, leave C4 in and short R4. The character of the sound can also be modified by splitting R3 into

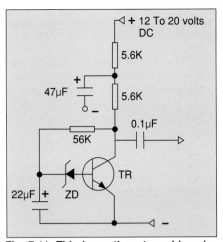

Fig. 7-11. This is another steam hiss circuit. It can drive an LM386 amplifier. It requires at least 12 volts.

two resistors of approximately equal value and connecting a 0.01µF capacitor to negative from their junction. The chuffs then sound more like a 2-10-4 than a 2-6-2.

There are three versions of the LM386 chip: LM386-N1 is rated at 6 volts; LM386-N3, 9 volts; and LM386-N4, 16 volts. I've specified LM386-N4. Don't use the -N1 or -N3 versions; check which one your suppliers offer if they call it just an LM386. At the time of writing Digi-Key listed only the -N1 and a Samsung LM386NKS (unspecified voltage), but could obtain the -N4 version. The -N4 was available from Electro Sonic in Toronto (phone 416-494-1555). Radio Shack has it as 276-1511, but it could be any version, so inspect the chip through the package.

Assembly

The circuit board and component

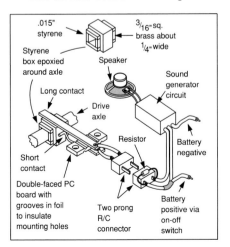

Fig. 7-13. Fabricating a steam sound cam switch with connections. The 220-ohm, 0.5-watt resistor maintains hiss from a stopped locomotive.

PARTS LIST FOR ZENER DIODE NOISE GENERATOR (FIG. 7-11)

TR	NPN small signal transistor, 2N2222A: Mouser 511-2N2222A; Digi-Key 2N2222APH
ZD	12-volt, 250- or 400-milliwatt Zener diode, 1N759, 1N963, or 1N5242: Mouser 333-1N5242B; Digi-Key 1N5242B
Resistors	Two 5.6K and one 56K, all 0.25-watt
Capacitors	Axial lead types facilitate assembly on the terminal strip. 47µF, 25-volt axial-lead electrolytic capacitor: Digi-Key (Panasonic) P6346; Mouser (Xicon) XA-14025V47 22µF, 25-volt axial-lead electrolytic capacitor: Digi-Key (Panasonic) P6344; Mouser (Xicon) XA-14025V22
Capacitor	Film, 0.1µF, 100-volt: Mouser (Xicon) 140-PF2A104J; Digi-Key (Panasonic) EF1104
Miscellaneous	Terminal strip for assembly with minimum of 8 tags: Mouser 153-2408, or use two 158-1007

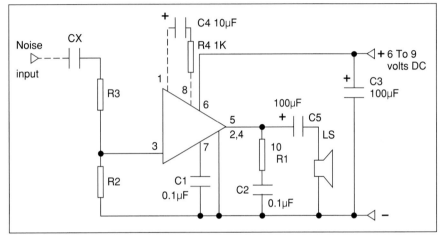

Fig. 7-12. The LM386-N4 amplifier can be driven from Zener diode or digital noise sources and is about as small as an amplifier gets.

layouts of fig. 7-16 show the amplifier with the MM5437N sound chip. If you use either of the other noise generators, omit the MM5437N socket and CX1 and CX2, and connect a jumper across where CX1 would be. You can also omit the DC positive and negative leads for the MM5437N and need not drill the holes for the device. Fig. 7-17 shows the three-IC noise board and the amplifier board (with the MM5437N fitted). The tender shown is

Fig. 7-14. The magnet on the inside of the tender wheel triggers the reed switch once per revolution.

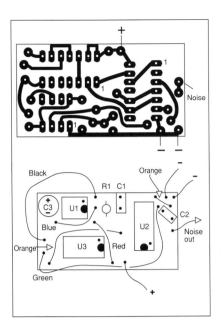

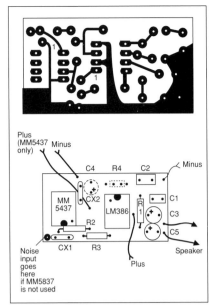

Fig. 7-15. (far left) Full-size PC board layout and component locations for digital steam hiss noise generator.

Fig. 7-16. (Left)Full-size PC board layout and component locations for amplifier and noise generator.

HO scale, and the speaker is 1¼" diameter, 8 ohms.

Insert the ICs last. The MM5437N is sensitive to static electricity; the LM386-N4 less so. Watch the IC pin locations and the polarity of C3, C4, and C5.

Fig. 7-18 shows the connections between the boards, speaker, battery, and the interrupter switch for chuff sound.

How can I synchronize the steam chuffs with the drive wheels?

Fig. 7-13 shows one method, a phosphor bronze switch that is opened and closed by driver rotation, interrupting the DC positive battery supply to the amplifier. This can be once, twice, or four times per driver revolution. I favor once per revolution of a tender wheel. Fig. 7-14 shows a magnet on a tender wheel that closes a reed switch.

Lionel currently uses a rotating magnet on a tender axle that triggers a Hall effect integrated circuit; this is the same principle as the electronic distributor used in many automobiles. Herkat of Germany uses a reflective switch: a combined infrared LED and photo transistor point to the plated inside face of a driver. Half the driver is covered with black paint, and as the driver turns, the light from the LED is reflected back to the photo transistor during half the rotation. The photo transistor acts as the switch. Fig. 7-19 shows the driver-operated switch on the axle of a Bachmann G scale 4-6-0. The two fingers of the switch are shorted twice per driver revolution. Other suggestions have included a phosphor bronze wiper rubbing against the inside of a driver. Segments of insulating tape or paint on the inside of the driver interrupt contact, at least until the paint or tape wears off.

Yet another method is to use a light shining on a CdS photocell. The

PARTS LIST FOR AMPLIFIER BOARD (FIG. 7-16)

R1	10-ohm, 0.25-watt resistor (brown black black)
R2	10K, 0.25-watt resistor (brown black orange)
R3	82K (gray red orange) or 1.0-megohm (brown black green), 0.25-watt resistor (see text)
R4	1K, 0.25-watt resistor (brown black red)—optional, see text
C1, C2	0.1µF, 50-volt multilayer capacitors: Mouser 21RZ310; Digi-Key (Panasonic) P4917
C3, C5	100µF, 10-volt electrolytic capacitors: Digi-Key (Panasonic) P6214; Mouser (Xicon) 140-XR10V100
C4	10µF, 10-volt electrolytic capacitor: Digi-Key (Panasonic) P5227; Mouser 140-XR10V10—optional, see text
CX1, CX2	0.047µF, 25-volt ceramic disk capacitors: Digi-Key (Panasonic) P4307; Mouser (Xicon) 140-CD50Z9-503Z—used only with the MM5437N IC
ICs	National Semiconductor MM5437N (not used with separate noise board, see text) and LM386-N4
Miscellaneous	One or two 8-pin IC sockets: Mouser 506-208-AG29D; Digi-Key A9208 PC board material 1" × 1⅞"
Speakers	8-ohm impedance: Digi-Key (Panasonic) P9601-ND (20mm dia.); P9503-ND (36mm dia.); P9610-ND (80mm dia.). Mouser (Kobitone) 25SP015 (1.5" dia.); 25RF122 (2.5" dia.); 25RF124 (3" dia.).

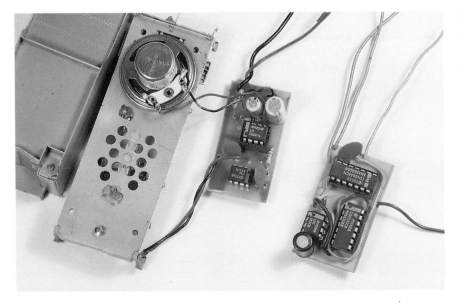

Fig. 7-17. The three-transistor noise generator board and amplifier board. The tender floor (showing the speaker sound holes) is HO.

light brightness is proportional to motor speed (it's connected across the throttle voltage), and thus the resistance of the CdS cell is inversely proportional to motor speed. The CdS cell is connected as the timing resistor in an IC timer. The output pulses of the timer speed up with the motor and are used to trigger the sound. I've used this in both steam and diesel sound applications; you can find the circuits in my other Kalmbach books.

For steam, the simple way is in my view the best: magnet and reed switch. If you don't have room for this, then the switch assembly of fig. 7-13 does the same thing. Note that the driver switch (or the reed switch if used) has a 220-ohm, 0.5-watt resistor connected across its contacts, and that the DC supply to the noise generator part is not switched by reed or driver switch. (Both are turned off by the on-off switch between them and the battery). This means that a hiss is in the speaker between chuffs, as the amplifier still gets a much reduced portion of power supply through the resistor. This lower-volume hiss is present even when the locomotive is stopped.

The reed switch charges C3 each time it is closed, and C3 holds a reserve of energy to keep the sound from decaying rapidly when the reed is in its off cycle. Thus there is a delayed attack and decay of the sound chuff. The effect is slight, but sounds more prototypical. An advantage of battery operation is that one side of the driver cam switch or the reed switch wiring can contact the locomotive chassis with no ensuing problem.

What about diesel sound?

There's a circuit in my Kalmbach book *Easy to Build Electronic Projects for Model Railroaders*. There was also a detailed design by Keith Gutierrez in the February through June 1991 issues of *Model Railroader*. Both circuits can be used for through-the-rails or around-the-layout sound. Kits of parts for Gutierrez' SDX-1 were available from CVP Products, P.O. Box 835772, Richardson, TX 75083.

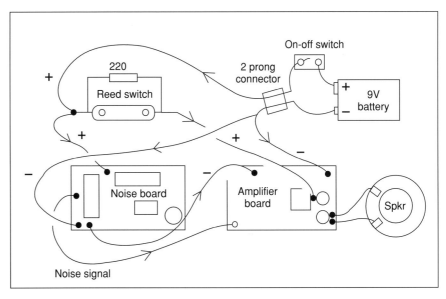

Fig. 7-18. Connections between amplifier, noise generator, battery, and chuff switch..

Fig. 7-19. The sound synchronization switch of a Bachmann G scale 4-6-0. The switch fingers short together twice per axle revolution.

8 The World of Model Railroad Electronics

IN THE PREVIOUS chapters I've covered the major categories of model railroad electronics. This final chapter covers most of the minor areas, some that have already been touched on and some that haven't. Most of the questions have arisen in letters and discussions with people in the hobby—and a few hobby store owners. I discuss, among other things, Hall effect devices, a super-flasher, high-frequency lighting, and the making of a FRED.

I also offer an answer to the question of what the electronics future will bring to us—which is often asked over the coffee cups and never answered correctly. Electronics and economics aren't sound-alikes for nothing!

How about some simple track control circuits using diodes?

To prevent a locomotive from crashing into the bumper stops at yard end, cut a gap in the left rail about a locomotive-length out from the end of track and connect a diode (1N5402) across the gap, pointing toward the end of the track. A locomotive will run into the gapped section and stop. When you flip the reversing switch, it can back out because the diode only conducts in one direction. If the result is the opposite of what it should be, reverse the diode. This simple diode circuit doesn't work with most command control throttles but is fine for all others.

You can also use diodes for an automatic slowing circuit, such as you might use through the diverging route of a facing-point turnout. Figure 8-1 shows the circuit. The south side of the track is positive for a train going east. Under these conditions the diodes in series with the sub-blocks on the south side of the track do not conduct, so the current for the train must first go through a 15-ohm resistor and then through a 50-ohm resistor. These give a substantial speed reduction. N scale or HO can motor users could probably double these resistor values, depending on the throttle voltage.

When the train travels in the opposite direction, almost the full throttle voltage is at the track and there is no automatic slowdown. A DPDT switch permits canceling of the automatic slowdown. Again 1N5402 diodes will suffice for motors of 3 amps or less. The resistors are available from Mouser: 5 watt, 28PR005-xx, where xx is the resistance in ohms; 10 watt, 28PR010-xx.

One of your earlier books had a stopping and starting circuit using an NTC resistor that is no longer available. What can I substitute?

An NTC resistor (Negative Temperature Coefficient) is also known as a thermistor. It has a fairly high resistance when cold, and its resistance drops when it is heated (usually by current passing through it). The original published circuit is in figure 8-2. Such a circuit is useful for partially automating the layout or perhaps on a trolley line that circles the town.

A train entering the block stops because of the resistance (cold) of the thermistor. As it sits at the station, the motor still draws current because power is applied, but the motor isn't getting enough voltage to turn it. The current through the motor heats up the thermistor, so the resistance drops until the train slowly restarts, gathers speed, and departs the block. The thermistor then cools down, ready for the next cycle.

NTC thermistors are made by Keystone Carbon Co., Thermistor Division, and Philips Components, Discrete Products Division. Newark

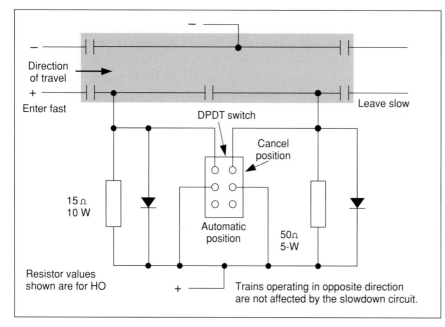

Direction of travel

Enter fast

Leave slow

DPDT switch

Cancel position

15 Ω 10 W

Automatic position

50 Ω 5-W

Resistor values shown are for HO

Trains operating in opposite direction are not affected by the slowdown circuit.

Fig. 8-1. Diodes used for automatic speed reduction.

Electronics distributes Keystone. Keystone CL-140 (Newark 81F3396) is a 50-ohm (cold), 1.1-amp device, and Keystone CL-90 (Newark 81F3393) is a 120-ohm (cold), 2-amp device. They are disks less than ½" in diameter. The Philips part number is 2322 642 7xxxx—the last four digits depend on value and tolerance. A 100-ohm, 20 percent thermistor should be sufficient. The Philips thermistor is a bolt-on device that can be secured to a small piece of aluminum for faster cooling.

The optional variable resistor in figure 8-2 can be a 50- or 100-ohm rheostat from a discarded power pack. Variable resistors are expensive, so in place of the variable resistor you might use a fixed resistor of 3 watts and 30 to 50 ohms (Mouser 28PR003-xx, where xx is the resistance in ohms).

The reason for using 16 volts AC and a diode (1N5402) to supply the stopping block is to guarantee restart. A low, normal-throttle voltage might not provide enough voltage even through a hot thermistor to restart the locomotive. Do not confuse the NTC resistor with a PTC (Positive Temperature Coefficient), which works in reverse—the resistance goes up when hot. Even dealers are sometimes confused!

Crossing-flasher circuits are either not adjustable for rate of flash or they are only for LEDs. Is there a universal circuit?

The Flexible Flasher is in figure 8-3. It has adjustable rates of flash for both sides, left and right independently. The rate of flash is independent of the supply voltage and is adjustable from 3 seconds off and 3 on to 90 flashes per minute. One side can be disconnected and the other will still flash with no damage or rate difference. The load can be up to 1 amp (many LEDs or several grain-of-wheat lamps); changes in the load don't affect the rate.

Electronically the circuit is simple. TR1 and TR2 form a multivibrator. When TR1 turns on it turns TR2 off, and vice versa. VR1 and VR2 together with C2 and C3 determine the rate at which each is on (or off). The small transistors drive two power transistors, TR3 and TR4. The Zener diode ZD and resistor R1 ensure that TR1 and TR2 get a fixed voltage supply

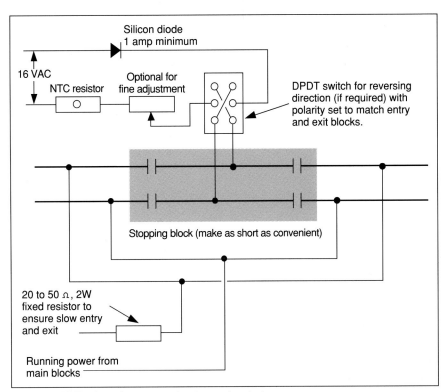

Fig. 8-2. NTC Resistor for automatic stop and restart.

regardless of the AC input voltage.

Assembly and testing

The PC board pattern and component positions are shown in figure 8-5. Watch the polarities of C1, C2, and C3 and the orientation of the four transistors. Rectifier D and Zener ZD must also be connected correctly (note the

Zener anode goes to negative, the reverse of a normal diode. Resistor R1 will get hot at higher AC input voltages. Mount it so that it does not touch the PC board.

If you connect the device to a 16-volt AC supply, the left and right lamp output voltage is sufficient to operate two grain-of-wheat incandescent

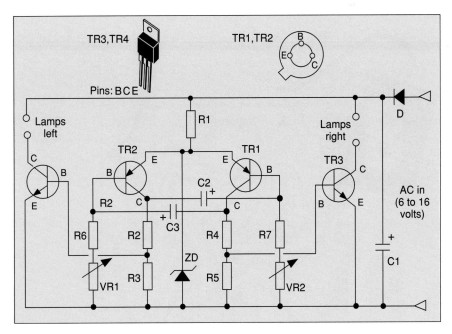

Fig. 8-3. Flash rate of this circuit is adjustable but unaffected by load, voltage, or heat. Lamps can be disconnected without damage to the unit.

Fig. 8-4. The Flexible Flasher.

lamps in series. The output voltage is too much for a single lamp. Crossing signals occur in pairs, one on the near side of the track and the other on the far side, so wire their left lamps in series and their right lamps in series. If a lower AC power supply is used (6 volts), use 470-ohm resistors for LEDs and connect GOW lamps individually, not in series pairs.

If one side flashes and not the other, check the connections of the side that is not flashing. If neither side flashes, check the voltage across the Zener diode—it should be 3.6 volts—and ensure that the Zener diode, C2, and C3 are connected in correct polarity. The lowest speed is set when the rotatable contacts of VR1 and VR2 are set to point outward. Adjustment for rate is separate for the two sides.

Instead of incandescents, individual light-emitting diodes can be used with 1K, 0.5-watt resistors connected in series with each LED or pair of LEDs themselves connected in series. The outer LED connections are positive, the inner connections on the board are negative (see Chapter 2 for how to connect LEDs).

My detection circuit works erratically. Is there a cure?

It's most likely that your motor brushes and commutator are worn, causing small sparks that create radio frequency transmissions, which in turn set up signals in your detector wiring. This also causes problems with on-board sound systems. Shielding the wiring will not help much, but adding at least one choke (coil) and a capacitor to the motor will. The best answer is to use new motors—and to add the coil and capacitor.

If you examine Bachmann G scale radio-controlled, sound-equipped locomotives, you'll find the motor has chokes in each brush lead and capacitors between each brush and the motor frame—not overkill at all, when you consider that the locomotive has two devices subject to interference.

You can make a choke by winding about 20 turns of fine copper wire on a pencil. Mouser (HiQ) 434-04-100M is a ready-made choke rated at 10 microhenries, 0.24 ohm, and 1.3 amps. It is

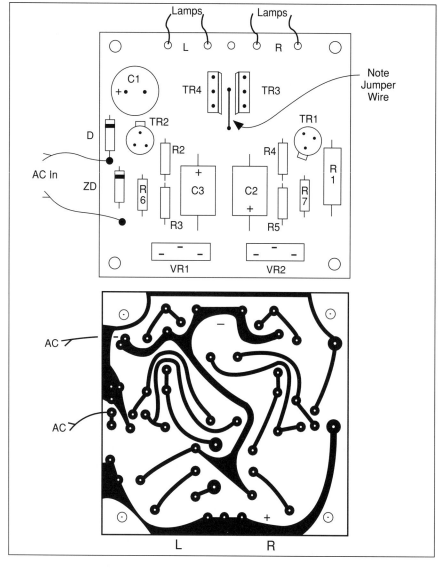

Fig. 8-5. Full-size PC board layout and component locations for Flexible Flasher.

Fig. 8-6. Eliminating motor interference. The capacitor is essential, but the coil may not be necessary.

0.6" long and 0.3" in diameter. A 50- or 100-volt ceramic disk capacitor should be sufficient. Fig. 8-6 shows connections and values.

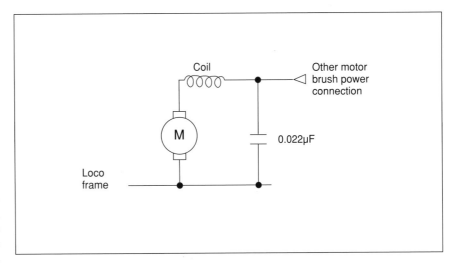

Should electronic devices for model railroads have electromagnetic interference shielding?

Computer equipment has EMI filters for two purposes: to keep external waveforms from disturbing the computer and to keep internal waveforms from disturbing other equipment. In general electronic devices for model railroads need no protection from external interference. The only item in this book that creates any is the SCR throttle of Chapter 4, and the amount is minuscule.

Laws change. What was considered safe electrically ten years ago is favored no longer; we may find that all equipment connected to line voltage will be required to have EMI reduction components sometime soon. An EMI filter is shown in figure 8-7. It has a line socket, and its output goes to the power transformer primary. It contains choke coils and capacitors. Mouser (Corcom) 538-1VB3 is a similar package for SCR and power supply equipment up to 3 amps at 117 volts AC.

Is there an electronic circuit for a FRED?

FRED is an acronym for Flashing Rear End Device, a gizmo that since 1982 has been hung on the rear coupler of the last car of more and more freight trains. It has two purposes: it transmits information about brakeline air pressure by radio to the engineer in the cab of the locomotive, and it is an end-of-train marker. It replaces the watchful eye of the conductor on the air-brake gauge in the caboose and the marker lamps on the rear of the caboose—and the caboose itself, since the conductor now rides up front with the engineer.

The circuit, shown in figure 8-8, uses very few components. The LM3909N is an 8-pin integrated circuit that works from as low as 1.5 volts. It steps up this voltage to about 2.5 to drive an LED, and it also contains the flasher circuitry. When I demonstrated the circuit there was

Fig. 8-7. Electromagnetic interference suppression components are wired between the AC line and the power transformer. In the future they may be required by law.

argument as to the rate of flash for a FRED, so I made the circuit adjustable to suit the critics—from less than 30 to more than 100 flashes per minute.

The circuit is battery-operated, but the average current draw is about 0.5 milliamp. If you switch the device off when you aren't operating your railroad, the battery should last a year. Figure 8-9 shows an AA battery, but AAA or N size batteries can be used to shorten the PC board to fit N scale boxcars. For O or G scale you can use a C or D battery, with a useful increase in car weight!

Assembly

The IC, the LED, capacitor C, and the battery must be inserted in the correct polarity—see figure 8-8. The longer lead of the LED is the positive connection. I fabricated a battery holder from scrap copper sheet, but

the parts list gives you off-the-shelf sources for one. The battery connections I made were screwed through the PC board to make mechanical contact with the copper foil. If you use a separate battery holder, you will need wires between holder and PC board. If you elect to use a shorter battery, simply trim off the left end of the PC board to fit.

The on-off switch is mounted to the underside of the PC board; the miniature toggle switch I used could be operated by a pencil point inserted through a hole in the bottom of the boxcar. You can wire any sort of hidden switch on wires to the PC board if you wish. The LED can also have its leads extended if required. I didn't use an IC socket because the LM3909N is not a CMOS static-sensitive type—but that doesn't mean you should abandon all anti-static care.

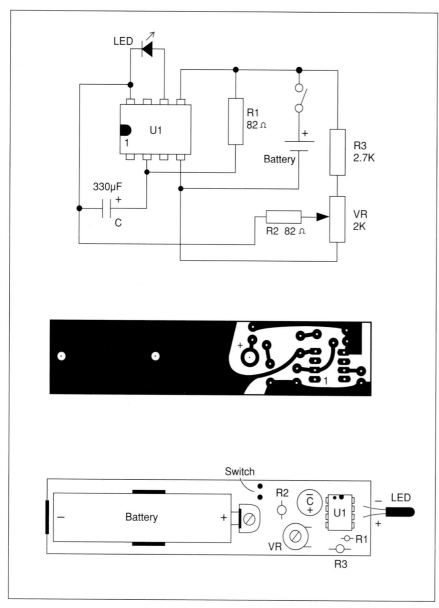

Fig. 8-8. Circuit, full-size PC board layout, and component locations for a FRED. With a smaller battery it will fit into an N scale car.

Our club acquired some capacitor discharge (CD) switch-machine power units that use an SCR, but they came without a wiring diagram. Can you advise?

Transistor CD units are more popular with suppliers. (Circuits for these are in Chapter 5). The SCR (Silicon Controlled Rectifier) circuit is shown in figure 8-10 and has the advantages of the transistor system—freedom from destruction of the switch machine solenoid coils and very rapid recharge time between uses. It also has the disadvantage common to both types—high current through the pushbutton switches when the switch machines are operated.

When the AC input is applied, the SCR turns on and charges the capacitor with DC (the SCR is a rectifier). The turn-on signal is applied to the gate (G) through D1 and the 820-ohm resistor. When either pushbutton is operated, the capacitor discharges its energy into the switch machine coil. If the pushbutton is held down, the SCR will not turn on and recharge the capacitor because the gate is then connected to the negative side of the capacitor. Only when the button is released can the capacitor again be recharged, and that happens almost instantly.

Figure 8-11 shows a unit assembled on a plastic panel using silicone sealant as adhesive. If more energy is required from this unit, the capacitor

can be increased to 3,300µF without any other changes to the circuit.

Should I convert to command control?

Command control systems allow independent operation of several trains without the need to isolate them electrically with block selector switches. The systems require an electronic receiver to be fitted to each locomotive. If you are prepared to modify your locomotives and go to the expense of the electronics, command control is worth considering. Layout wiring, though greatly reduced, is not eliminated, and short circuits can still be a problem. Some commercial command control systems can put enough power into the track to melt code 40 rail under extreme conditions! Figure 8-12 shows a photo of an early commercial CTC-16 receiver. Because of the number of components the PC board is double-sided; there are copper traces on both sides of the board—hard to make at home.

Choose your supplier carefully; only two or three manufacturers have offered consistent quality and realistic warranty programs. An article in the July 1993 issue of Model Railroader (pages 88-93) reviewed comercial command control systems.

I suggest you try a system on a friend's layout before deciding, and be aware of drawbacks such as being unable to send sound through the rails. Command control requires an investment in time and money, but the result could be just what you want.

How do electronic track cleaners work? Are they effective?

High-frequency high-voltage current can break down small patches of grime, dirt, and oxidation between rails and wheel treads. The frequency is usually around 250 kilohertz; the pulsing voltage is about 350 volts. It doesn't give a shock because essentially it is like static electricity but at a lower voltage. The track cleaner is operational only when throttle current is not flowing—when a locomotive is not present or when a locomotive is present and the track is dirty. Track cleaners shut off automatically whenever the track is clean and a locomotive or a lighted car is on the rails. There is no chance of damaging lights and motors because if they are working, the high voltage is not present.

Fig. 8-9. FRED unit with HO scale boxcar.

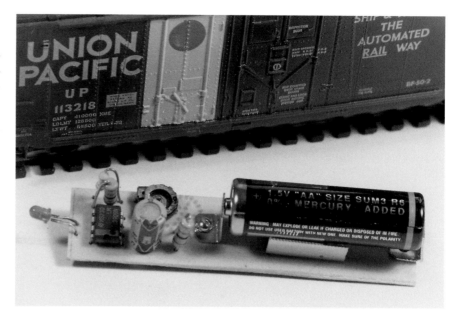

Fig. 8-9. FRED unit with HO scale boxcar.

The electronic track cleaners can't be used with Twin-T detectors, sound through the rails, or command control systems. They must also be kept disconnected from reversing loops because the wiring can cause track shorts. Any leakage across the tracks will also cause the safety shutoff to function. They operate with fewer problems if both rails are gapped; with common-rail wiring the high frequency can disappear through the common connection with the other cabs. Alternately each cab can have its own track cleaner permanently wired to it.

Their main utility? Heavy smokers with conventional layouts should find them a boon, and the electronic tickle across the rails should keep your cat off the layout!

Is there an up-to-date circuit for a high-frequency lighting generator?

Command control, which places a constant voltage across the rails, and simple diode circuits have cut the demand for high-frequency constant-lighting generators. The original purpose of such a unit was to provide high-frequency power to the track to light passenger rolling stock and loco-motive headlamps independently of track power. My first book, *Practical Electronic Projects for Model Rail-roaders* (published by Kalmbach in 1974 and long out of print), included a supersonic-frequency generator (SSF), but the idea had been around since at least 1950.

The SSF generator complicated layout wiring. The locomotive motor is unaffected by high-frequency AC and offers a high resistance to it. The lamps see no difference between SSF and track DC, and light from both. Lamps could burn out from the additive power of SSF and DC, so a small capacitor (0.22μF) was usually added in series with each lamp on the train to block track power and pass the SSF to light the bulbs. The SSF also had to be transferred across rail block gaps with a 1.0μF capacitor.

However, an SSF generator can be of use in engine terminals and stations so that standing locomotives and pas-

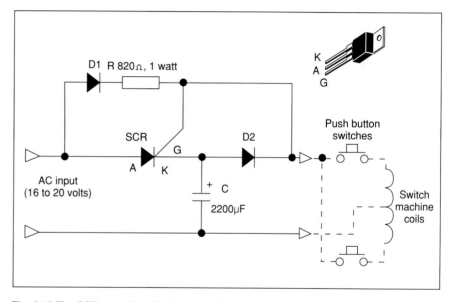

Fig. 8-10 The SCR capacitor discharge switch-machine power supply recharges quickly

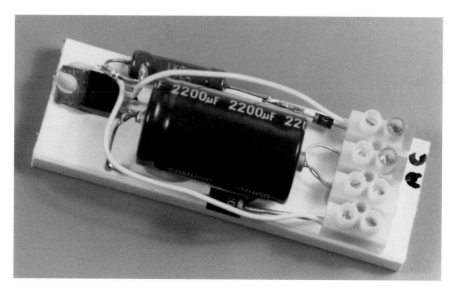

Fig. 8-11. The SCR capacitor discharge unit.

nent layout are in figure 8-15. Compared with earlier circuits, this one has an extra transistor (TR1), which is a phase shift oscillator. It determines the frequency of oscillation (35 kilohertz) and provides a positive feedback path.

The unit is fed 16 volts AC from a spare power pack. It must not be the power pack that supplies train power, because in most power packs there is a common connection between one side of the variable DC and the fixed AC terminals. The power drawn is only 0.5 amp maximum, and if no lamps are burning the current is less than 50 milliamps.

The rectifier and filter capacitor wiring constitute a DC voltage doubler to ensure adequate SSF output voltage.

The components that must be assembled in correct polarity are D1, D2, D3, C1, C2, TR1, TR2, and TR3. Bolt TR2 and TR3 to the heat sinks with their metal side to the sink and with a smear of thermally conductive silicone grease between the two metal surfaces. No insulation is used, so both heat sinks are at the collector voltage of the respective transistor; take care that the metal does not therefore contact D3, R7, and R8, which are close by. Ensure that the correct resistors are in the area between TR2 and C2. There are three different values in close proximity, and if any of them is incorrect the unit will not operate.

Test the unit with a grain-of-wheat lamp across the two output connections. It should light at good brightness with 16-volt AC input. If it doesn't, check that there is 35 to 40 volts DC from positive to negative (marked in figure 8-14). If there isn't, the likely culprit is D1, D2, C1, or C2. Check also for 17 to 20 volts DC from negative to the junction of C8 and C9. If it isn't there, check the values of R4, R5, and R6; also that TR1 is inserted correctly (the E connection is closest to the tab on the metal case).

Connecting the SSF unit to the layout

See figure 8-16. The only alteration to existing wiring is the addition of a choke between the cab selector switch and the gapped side of the

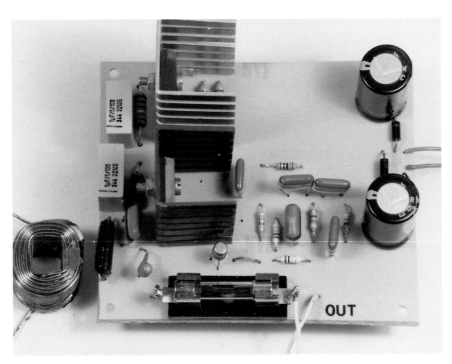

Fig. 8-13. The SSF lighting generator keeps locomotive and car lights lit independently of throttle voltage.

senger cars can have their lights on. What I suggest with the circuit that follows is to have the SSF only in those blocks where the normal running voltage is low or turned off. There is no need to modify the existing light wiring in the rolling stock; the normally supplied 12- to 16-volt lamps are left in place.

If the SSF is only moderately high, say the equivalent of 10 volts DC, then 6 to 8 volts of throttle voltage can be added, enough to pull the locomotives in and out of the SSF-lit blocks without lamp overload. This also simplifies the chokes needed to keep SSF out of

the throttles; I simply add one choke in series with the non-common rail side of each SSF-lit block. No modification to the throttles is needed.

SSF lighting is not compatible with sound through the rails, command control, and TWIN-T track detectors. However, if it is used only in special-purpose blocks—engine terminal and station—the rest of the layout can have sound and detectors.

SSF Lighting Generator

The circuit in figure 8-14 can light up to 10 grain-of-wheat bulbs. The full-size PC board pattern and compo-

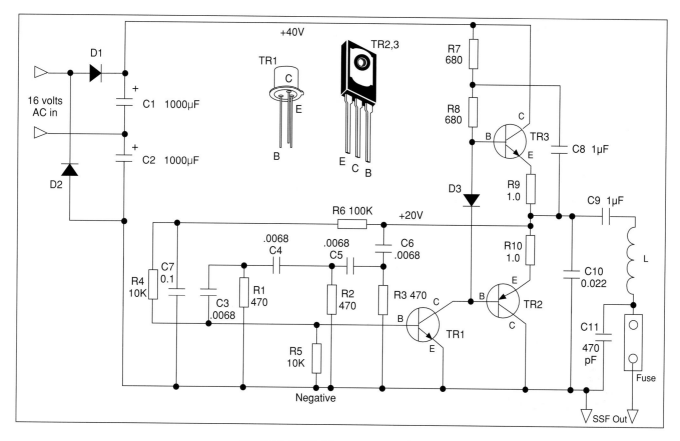

Fig. 8-14. SSF lighting generator circuit.

track. This choice keeps SSF voltage from disappearing through the throttle when either cab is connected. I recommend that a control-panel on-off switch be connected in series with one AC input lead

The SSF unit may fail to give output with a heavy load of lamps. Turning the on-off switch off and on again usually resolves this. The 1-amp fuse protects against track shorts; a heavy lamp load will not cause the fuse to blow. However, if the unit fails to operate, check this fuse.

Are Hall Effect devices useful to model railroaders?

Most Hall Effect devices are much like small plastic-case transistors that can be switched on by the presence of a magnetic field. So far as we are concerned they are similar to a reed switch but smaller. While reed switches need no separate power supply, the Hall effect devices do. Hall Effect devices have no memory. If power is shut off, all positions will be off when power is turned on again.

One class of Hall device is different—the magnetic latch. The Hall switch is on only in the presence of a magnetic field, and it turns off when

the field moves away, but the Hall latch turns on in a magnetic field of one polarity and stays on until a magnetic field of the opposite polarity appears. This can be of use as a train detector if the locomotive carries a disk magnet with north pole down, and the last item of rolling stock has a disk magnet with the south pole down. The first magnet passing over the Hall device turns it on and the last magnet turns it off. No track connections are needed, so in essence this can provide a foolproof, bidirectional signal system. The difficult part is where to mount the magnets, particularly the one at the end of the train—but if all your trains carry a caboose or observation car, that problem is solved.

Hall devices are made by Allegro Microsystems (which used to be called Sprague Semiconductor when it was owned by Penn Central) and Texas Instruments. Products of both manufacturers are distributed by Newark Electronics.

The circuits in figure 8-17 illustrate the Allegro UGN3120U Hall detector directly driving a SPDT (1 Form C) relay or driving the relay via an NPN transistor. The UGN3120U is not sensitive to magnet strength and

is tolerant of the separation between magnet and the detector.

The UGN3120U is only on when it is covered by the magnet; the UGN3075U is on with one polarity of magnet and stays on until a magnet of the opposite polarity arrives. Because these devices have a low current output, the relay used for direct drive must be of a high resistance. For 24 volts, the Omron G5L-112P-PS-DC24 (Digi-Key Z722-ND) is suitable. For 12 volts the relay is less critical because of the TIP29 transistor driver (Omron G5L-112P-PS-DC12, Digi-Key Z721-ND). Both UGNs are listed in the 1993 Newark catalog.

Model aircraft can be controlled by radio—why not trains?

Model plane radio control systems can of course be applied to model trains. The servos can be connected mechanically to a transistor throttle—and there you go! You still need to finger the control panels for route and block selection if you control more than one locomotive and one piece of track. Ideally the radio receiver will be powered from the throttle (with an appropriate regulated power supply—see Chapter 3) to avoid depending on a

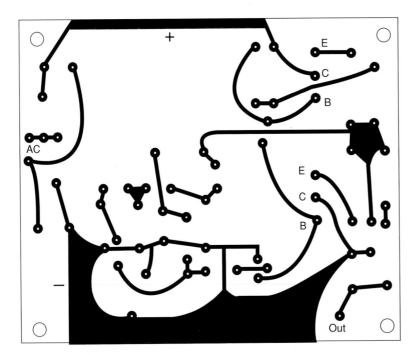

Fig. 8-15. Full-size PC board layout and component locations for SSF lighting generator.

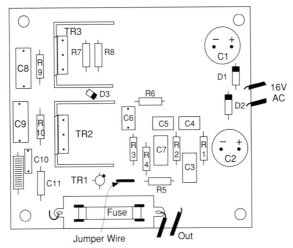

battery. A DPDT relay can act to replace the reversing switch.

Several circuits of this nature have been published. Andy Sperandeo had one in *Railroad Model Craftsman* in December 1978; the principles are unchanged. In the March and April 1983 issues of *Model Railroader* Keith Gutierrez described how to fit a Futaba radio control unit to his CTC-16 command control system, including a discussion of where to put the antenna and how to disguise it. An earlier book of mine, *34 New Electronic Projects for Model Railroaders*, showed how to adapt for model railroad use a radio-controlled toy that used LM1871N and LM1872N integrated circuits.

Bachmann's G scale radio-controlled Big Hauler 4-6-0 has plastic drive wheels and runs on 9 volts' worth of C batteries. The electronics includes radio-controlled throttle and synchronized sound. The transmitter has a single slide control with speed control and direction reverse at each end. The receiver measures 1½" × 4⅜" × 1", so it will fit inside an HO boxcar. The antenna is again a problem—it's a folded whip inside the rather large cab of the locomotive. The transmitter and receiver are simple circuits that don't compare with the LM1871/1872 circuit for sensitivity and range; on the plus side, of course, you don't need a license to operate the system. Bachmann says the control range of the Big Hauler is 20 feet; I've used the LM1871/1872 at over 35 feet.

If you convert the Bachmann radio control system to use a track-powered motor, use a low-current can motor to avoid overloading the transistors in the receiver. For all radio receivers and throttles that are on the locomotive or in an attached car, special care is needed to suppress motor interference with capacitors and chokes (see fig. 8-6).

What size connecting wire should I use?

The size depends on the length and the amount of current. Table 8-1 gives

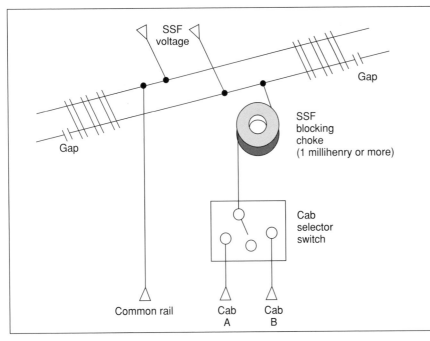

Fig. 8-16. SSF lighting requires a choke between the block selector switch and the track for each block.

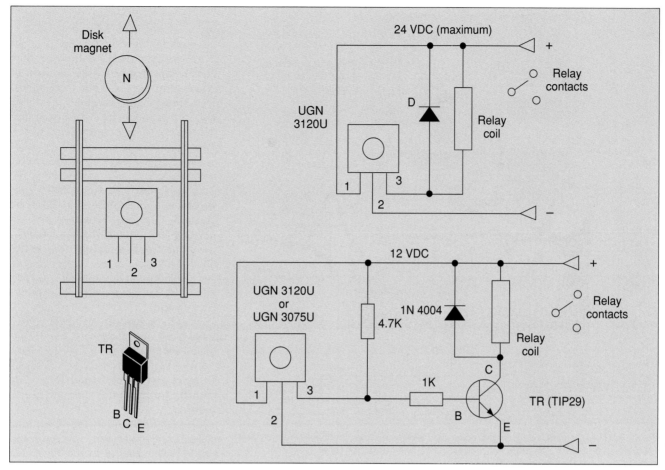

Fig. 8-17. Hall effect magnetic switch circuits. The magnet must be polarized from surface to surface, not crosswise (like Kadee uncoupler magnets).

a good idea of wire gauges to use. The ohms-per-100-feet column allows calculation of possible voltage drop with current. According to the venerable Ohm's Law, 1 ohm of resistance drops 1 volt at 1 amp—or 4 volts at 4 amps or 8 volts at 8 amps. Taking a typical model-railroad-length piece of wire as an example, 10 feet of 20AWG would drop only 0.5 volt at 5 amps (the table indicates 5.1 volts loss for 100 feet). That size would be a good choice for block wiring for all scales. For N, even 26AWG would be acceptable (0.5 amp would drop 2 volts over 100 feet, or 0.5 volt over 25 feet).

For layout lighting 26 AWG should be fine for everything except flood lights! Each grain-of-wheat lamp draws 20 to 60 milliamps; 16 lamps will draw no more than 1 amp maximum.

Solenoid switch machines draw heavy short-term currents, up to 10 amps per unit. You should use 14AWG or 16AWG for all but the shortest runs, (14AWG is the standard household power wiring gauge, available as 2/14 in any hardware store). For DC motor-drive switch machines, which draw about 0.5 amp, use 26AWG.

Is there a light detector that can drive a relay directly?

Light is more difficult to use as a sensor driver than a magnet. Light has many variables—time of day, overhead lights, and spaces between cars. Figure 8-18 shows Allegro Microsystems' ULN-3330T (available from Newark Electronics) operating an Omron G5L-112P-PS-DC12 relay (Digi-Key Z721-ND). The relay is energized when the sensor surface is shadowed. The ULN-3330 turns on when light falls below 5 lumens per square foot. For comparison, twilight is about 1 lumen per square foot and an overcast day is about 100 lumens per square foot.

Note the arrangement of the overhead light to avoid light gaps between rolling stock; the relay is de-energized as soon as light is re-established. The detector can be rendered less sensitive to ambient light by partly covering its surface or shielding it from side light.

The circuit has memory; when power is switched off and then on again, the circuit will read the same as when power was switched off. The resistance of the relay coil must not be less than 300 ohms (the Omron relay specified is 360 ohms), and the circuit voltage must not exceed 15 volts DC.

What about fiber optics for lighting?

Although very small incandescent lamps and LEDs are available, there are still uses for fiber-optic "light pipes" to transmit light around corners and into narrow places. (Don't confuse relatively inexpensive plastic fiber light conduits with sophisticated telecommunications fiber optics.) Acrylic moldings are used in many locomotives to conduct light from a single lamp to the number boards at front and rear. If a model doesn't offer this facility, it's easier to add fiber-optic light guides than attempt to fabricate an acrylic molding—and more light is transferred.

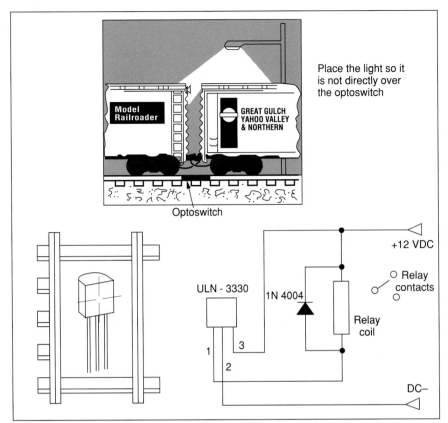

Place the light so it is not directly over the optoswitch

Optoswitch

ULN - 3330

1N 4004

+12 VDC

Relay contacts

Relay coil

DC−

Fig. 8-18. The optoswitch sensor energizes the relay when it is shadowed from ambient or overhead light.

Fig. 8-19. Fiber-optic light guides are an ideal way to send light to tight places. The ends of the fibers can be cut, filed, and polished as required.

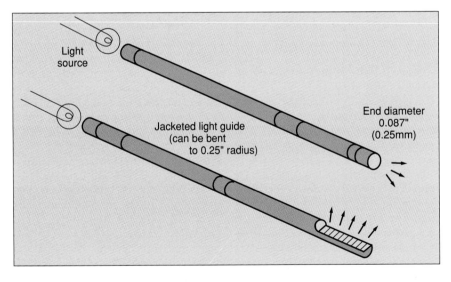

Light source

Jacketed light guide (can be bent to 0.25" radius)

End diameter 0.087" (0.25mm)

Figure 8-19 shows how the light guide can be cut, filed, and polished at the ends for head or tail lights or for illuminating number boards. The same shapes can be used for yard or street lights or even for table lamps seen through the windows of a cafe. The light source can be an incandescent lamp or a bright LED of any color. Light transmission can be yards in length if you don't try to include too many bends.

Plastic-covered fiber optic light guides are available from Edmund Scientific Company. Examples are:

• D2504, outside diameter 0.087"; minimum bending radius 0.25" (multifiber strand)

• D2506, outside diameter 0.119"; minimum bending radius 0.5" (multifiber strand)

• D2536, outside diameter 0.087"; minimum bending radius 0.775" (mono-strand)

Is there anything dramatic coming up in model railroad electronics?

Model Railroader asked six men considered experts in the field and printed their replies in the November 1990 issue. Most of the predictions were in the field of command control and computer systems; better sound systems were also a subject of discussion.

I anticipate better and smaller sound units; removal of train power from the track completely, relying on efficient batteries and motors; and control from a digitally modulated antenna system under the rails—no stalling, no shorts, no wiring nightmares!

Well, there you have it. Everything is either under way or possible. What's missing? Investment in design and manufacturing. Until then look for spin-offs from the electronics of—to take two extremes—toys and automobiles!

FIG. 8-20—WIRE SIZES AND CHARACTERISTICS

Wire size AWG	Diameter (inches)	Copper Ohms per 100 feet 68° F	Safe current in amperes in closed space	Nichrome Ohms per foot	Wire size AWG	Diameter (inches)	Copper Ohms per 100 feet 68° F	Safe current in amperes in closed space	Nichrome Ohms per foot
12	0.080	0.16	15	0.092	22	0.025	1.61	4	0.936
14	0.064	0.25	13	0.146	24	0.020	2.57	3	1.49
16	0.051	0.40	10	0.233	26	0.016	4.08	2	2.37
18	0.040	0.64	8	0.370	28	0.013	6.49	1.5	3.76
20	0.032	1.02	5	0.589	30	0.010	10.3	1.3	5.98

SUPPLIERS

Advance Transformer Co.
O'Hare International Center, 10275 West Higgins Road, Rosemont, IL 60018; phone 709-390-5000

Allegro Microsystems Inc.
363 Plantation St., Worcester, MA 01605; phone 508-795-1300

C&K Components Inc.
15 Riverdale Ave., Newton, MA 02158-1082; phone 617-964-6400

CW Industries
130 James Way, Southampton, PA 18966; phone 215-355-7080

Datak Products
55 Freeport Blvd., No. 23, Sparks, NV 89431; phone 702-359-7474

DC Electronics
P. O. Box 3203, Scottsdale, AZ 85271

Dialight Corporation
1913 Atlantic Ave., Manasquan, NJ 08736; phone 908-223-9400

Digi-Key Corporation
phone 800-344-4539; free catalog

Edmund Scientific Co.
101 E. Gloucester Pike, Barrington, NJ 08007-1380; phones 609-573-6858 for information, 609-573-6250 to place orders; catalog available

EG&G
10900 Page Blvd., St. Louis, MO 63132; phone 314-423-4900

Electronics Components Group
26 N. Fifth St., Minneapolis, MN 55403; phone 612-375-9639

Electro Sonic
Toronto, ON, Canada
phone 416-494-1555

Hamlin Inc.
612 E. Lake St., Lake Mills, WI 53551; phone 414-648-3000 (products are sold only through distributors, not directly)

Hammond Electronics
1690 Walden Ave., Buffalo, NY 14225-4971; phone 716-894-5710

Hasco Components International Corp.
247-40 Jericho Turnpike, Bellrose Village, NY 11001; phone 516-328-9292

Hewlett-Packard Components
Customer Information Center, Building 49 AV, 19310 Pruneridge Ave., Cupertino, CA 95014

ITT Components
5 Jenner St., Irvine, CA 92718; phone 714-727-3001

Jameco Electronics
1355 Shoreway Rd., Belmont, CA 94002; phone 415-592 8097; free catalog

Jerome Industries Corp.
730 E. Division St., Elizabeth, NJ 07201

Keystone Carbon Co.
Thermistor Division, 1935 State Street, St. Marys, PA 15857; phone 814-781-1591

Marktech
5 Hemlock St., Latham, NY 12110; phone 518-786-6591

Miniatronics Corp.
561K Acorn Street, Deer Park, NY 11749; phone 516-242-6464; fax 516-242-7796

Mouser Electronics
phone 800-992-9943; free catalog. Mouser offers same-day shipping, credit card and FAX ordering, and levies no handling charge for orders over $20.

National Semiconductor Corp.
2900 Semiconductor Dr., Box 58090, Santa Clara, CA 95052-8090; phone 408-721-5000

Newark Electronics
offices in most states; Chicago office phone 312-989-7800

NKK Switches
7850 E. Gelding Dr., Scottsdale, AZ 85260; phone 602-991-0942

Ocean State Electronics
P. O. Box 1458, Westerly, RI 02891

Philips Components
Discrete Products Divison, P. O. Box 760, Mineral Wells, TX 76067; phone 817-325-7871

Philips ECG Inc.
Distributor and Special Markets Division, 1025 Westminster Dr., P. O. Box 3277, Williamsport, PA 17701; phone 717-323-4691

Raychem Corporation
300 Constitution Dr., Menlo Park, CA 94025-1164; phone 415-361-3863

Texas Instruments Inc
P. O. Box 809066, Dallas, TX 75380-9066; phone 214-995-2011

Model Railroader and *Electronics Now* magazines' advertisers are also an excellent source for components.

Index